CORE ADVAI

MW01285439

Making Sense of
Conversions

Between Fractions, Decimals, and Percentages

DR. RANDY PALISOC

IRONBOX®
Education

IRONBOX®
Education

Contents

Essential Background Information

Making Sense of Conversions

Fraction

Decimal ⟷ Percentage

About the Author

My name is Dr. Randy Palisoc, and I'm on a mission to give kids **Power Over Numbers** and **Power Over Learning.**

I am a former classroom teacher, and I was a founder of the **five-time national award winning** Synergy Academies, whose elementary school was named the **#1 Urban Elementary School in America** by the National Center for Urban School Transformation in 2013.

The reason I designed this system is that too many students do not have a strong foundation in math, and they do not "get" the standard explanations found in many textbooks. This is troubling because students who struggle early on are often unable catch up to their peers later in life.

On the other hand, students who do have strong foundations have a greater shot at success later in life. In 2013, for example, students who were with Synergy since elementary school (all minority students) had a 95% pass rate on the California High School Exit Exam, compared to only about 79% statewide (all ethnicities).

As shown above, **strong foundations really do matter.**

The Core Advantage math fluency system by Ironbox Education is designed to build those foundations and to build fluency as quickly and as easily as possible. It does so by thinking like kids and teaching in a way that makes sense to them.

I designed this math fluency system based on my experience working with thousands of students from elementary school through high school and finding out what makes them successful. I hope you are able to use this system to give your students or children Power Over Numbers™ and Power Over Learning™!

Dr. Randy Palisoc received his Bachelor of Science degree from the University of Southern California (USC), his Master of Education degree from the University of California, Los Angeles (UCLA), and his Doctor of Education degree from USC.

The Power of Conversions

The ability to convert creates the ability to choose.

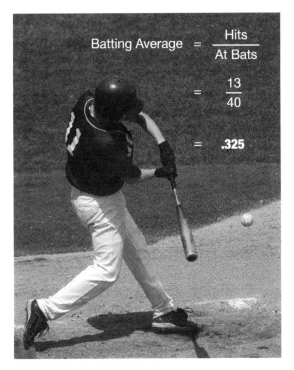

$$\text{Batting Average} = \frac{\text{Hits}}{\text{At Bats}}$$

$$= \frac{13}{40}$$

$$= .325$$

In math, numbers take on many different forms. For example, a single value such as 75% can be expressed not just in the form of a **percentage,** but also in the form of a **decimal** or in the form of a **fraction.** There is great power in knowing how to change a value from one form to another. It makes everything from tipping at a restaurant to comparing batting averages easier.

Unfortunately, many students struggle with these conversions, and as a result, they can't take advantage of the power behind these numbers. This is how this unit can help.

Making Sense of Conversions is one of the most important units in the Core Advantage series. Not only will is show students *how* to convert between fractions, decimals, and percentages, but also *why* it makes sense to do so.

Use this entire unit from beginning to end as designed, and students will not only know how convert numbers into different forms, but they'll gain the **power to choose which form works best.**

How does this system work?

First things first.

In order to do keep up with this unit, students must be fluent with their multiplication and division facts, with fractions, and with proportions. If students are not solid with these skills, go through the following four units first:

- *10 Powerful Steps to Multiplication Fluency*
- *Making Sense of Division*
- *Making Sense of Fractions*
- *Making Sense of Proportions*

  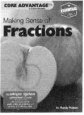 

The Core Advantage series is different from ordinary workbooks. The lessons begin with students working interactively on a short, easy-to-understand lesson with their teacher or their parent. The reason for this is that when students (especially young students) work with an actual person, it makes learning a much more personal and meaningful experience. **The human touch matters.**

It's important for teachers or parents to watch the lesson-by-lesson demo videos. This way, they'll know the key nuances to point out, and it takes the guesswork and confusion out of the lesson. There are also fully-annotated answer keys that not only show the answer, but also show the steps involved in getting there.

Each lesson provides students with well-thought-out, purposeful practice to promote fluency, and all the lessons build systematically upon each other. The following page provides a suggested pacing plan, and you can adjust the pacing as needed.

Pacing: Making Sense of Conversions

In this unit, students will be converting between fractions, decimals, and percentages. **Making Sense of Conversions** builds heavily upon the four prior units:

- *10 Powerful Steps to Multiplication Fluency*
- *Making Sense of Division*
- *Making Sense of Fractions*
- *Making Sense of Proportions*

Therefore, make sure students have successfully completed these previous units first.

Below is a sample pacing plan.

	Monday	Tuesday	Wednesday	Thursday	Friday
Week 1	BEGINNING OF PART 1 Lesson 1 Comparing Fractions Lesson 2 Converting Fractions to Percentages	Lesson 3 Converting Fractions, Decimals, and Percentages	Lesson 4 Converting Fractions, Decimals, and Percentages	Lesson 5 Converting Decimals and Percentages to Fractions	Lesson 6 Batting Averages
Week 2	Lesson 7 All Conversions Lesson 8 All Conversions	Lesson 9 The Power to Choose	BEGINNING OF PART 2 Efficiency Lesson A Computational Efficiency Efficiency Lesson B Simplifying Subtraction with Zeroes	Efficiency Lessons C and D Trailing zeroes Efficiency Lesson E Trailing Zeroes	Efficiency Lesson F Calculating 15% Easily Without Multiplying Efficiency Lesson G Hanging Zeroes
Week 3	Lesson 10 Markups vs. Markdowns Lesson 11 Tax and Tip	Lesson 12 Review of Key Conversions Lesson 13 Single Markup Problems	Lesson 14 Single Markdown Problems Lesson 15 One-Year Simple Interest	Lesson 16 Multiple Markups	Lesson 17 Multiple Markdowns
Week 4	Lesson 18 Markdowns Followed by Markups	Lesson 19 Simple vs. Compound Interest	Lesson 20 Simple vs. Compound Interest		

Addressing State Learning Standards or the Common Core State Standards

Today, schools across America are either using their own state's learning standards or the Common Core State Standards.

No matter what learning standards a school is using, this system helps give students an academic advantage by building fluency faster than has been possible in the past. Fluency is important for all students because it helps them be more precise, which in turn helps them more easily make sense of math.

Take a look at these two Standards for Mathematical Practice (MP), which are used by states using the Common Core State Standards:

> MP #1: Make sense of problems and persevere in solving them.
> MP #6: Attend to precision.

How do these two math practices go together?

- If students **cannot** attend to precision (#6), then they will not make sense of problems (#1), and they will not persevere in solving them (#1).

On the other hand,

- If students **can** attend to precision (#6), then they are more likely to make sense of problems (#1) and are more likely to persevere in solving them (#1).

As you can see, attending to precision (#6) can mean the difference between confidence and confusion.

The unique Core Advantage system used in this book can help give students an academic advantage in a short amount of time. It is designed to build fluency so that students can attend to precision (#6) and actually understand what they're doing in math.

It does take hard work and practice on the part of students, and only students themselves can determine their level of success based on their effort. The good news is that the greater their level of fluency, the more confidence students will have, and the more likely they are to persevere and put in that necessary hard work and practice.

Fluency matters, and I hope that you are able to use this system to build that fluency with your students.

-- Dr. Randy Palisoc

Part 1

Making Sense of
Conversions

Go down your *Success Tracker* in the order shown below and write your score for each of the activities as you complete them. The goal is to make any corrections necessary to earn a score of 100%.

Lesson	Lesson Name	Score
KEY LESSON 1	Comparing Fractions	
2	Converting Fractions to Percentages	
3	Converting Fractions, Decimals, and Percentages	
4	Converting Fractions, Decimals, and Percentages	
5	Converting Decimals and Percentages to Fractions	
KEY LESSON 6	Batting Averages	
7	All Conversions	
8	All Conversions	
KEY LESSON 9	The Power to Choose	

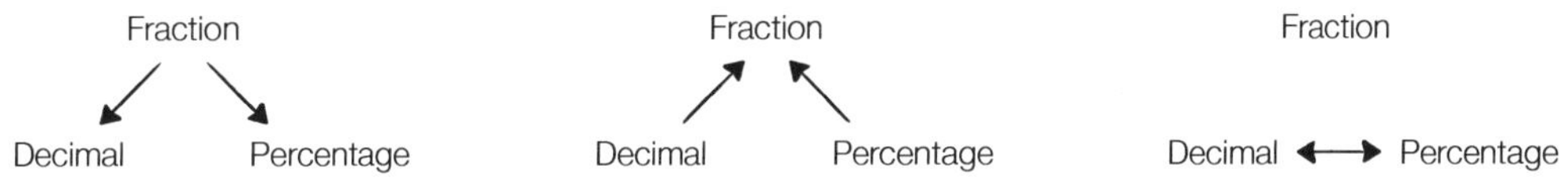

Fraction
↙   ↘
Decimal   Percentage

Fraction
↗   ↖
Decimal   Percentage

Fraction

Decimal ⟷ Percentage

Making Sense of Conversions | © ironboxeducation.com | **Teachers: Log in for demo videos.**

Name_____

Lesson 1: Comparing Fractions

Part I: List the factors of 100 (in pairs and in the correct order).

```
100

____ · ____

____ · ____

____ · ____

____ · ____

____ · ____
```

Part 2: Follow along with your instructor to complete this lesson.

Ana, Betty, Christy, Daisy, Emily, and Francine take six different tests, and they earned the scores shown below.

	Ana	Betty	Christy	Daisy	Emily	Francine
Score	$\frac{3}{4}$	$\frac{1}{2}$	$\frac{7}{10}$	$\frac{14}{20}$	$\frac{20}{25}$	$\frac{39}{50}$
A. Number Correct						
B. Number Wrong						
C.	With your partner, decide which student above has the highest grade. Defend your answer.					
D. Find the scores if they had taken the same 100-question test.						
E.	Who had the highest score? _____ Who had the lowest score? _____ Who had the same score? _____ and _____ Why is it now easier to answer these questions? _____					
F. Convert (with your teacher)	___ ___ ___ ___ ___ ___ ___ ____ ___	___ ___ ___ ___ ___ ___ ___ ____	Write only the percentage.	Write only the percentage.	Write only the percentage.	Write only the percentage.

A _____ is simply a _____ out of _____ (_____).

Fraction
↘
Decimal   Percentage

Lesson 2: Converting Fractions to Percentages

Part I: Factoring. List the factors of 100 (in pairs and in the correct order).

100

_____ · _____

_____ · _____

_____ · _____

_____ · _____

_____ · _____

Part 2: Use proportions to convert fractions to percentages.

A. $\dfrac{41}{50}$	B. $\dfrac{3}{100}$	C. $\dfrac{7}{10}$ Use the hanging zeroes shortcut.	D. $\dfrac{6}{25}$
E. $\dfrac{17}{20}$	F. $\dfrac{1}{2}$	G. $\dfrac{1}{4}$ Think: One quarter = _____	H. $\dfrac{2}{5}$
I. $\dfrac{9}{10}$ Use the hanging zeroes shortcut.	J. $\dfrac{3}{50}$	K. $\dfrac{30}{100}$	L. $\dfrac{24}{25}$
M. $\dfrac{10}{20}$	N. $\dfrac{1}{10}$	O. $\dfrac{3}{5}$	P. $\dfrac{4}{5}$
Q. $\dfrac{3}{4}$	R. $\dfrac{1}{5}$	S. $\dfrac{5}{10}$	T. $\dfrac{2}{4}$

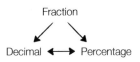

Lesson 3: Converting Fractions, Decimals and Percentages

Part 1: Label the missing place values names of the digits in: 3,259.648

	3	,	2	5	9	.	6	4	8
				10s	1s				

→

Part 2: Follow along with your instructor.

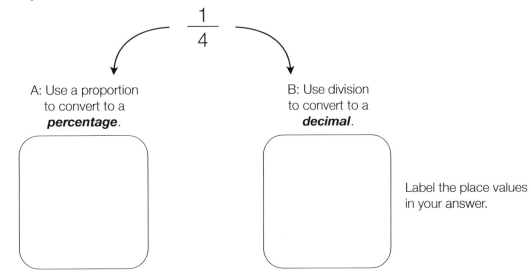

$$\frac{1}{4}$$

A: Use a proportion to convert to a ***percentage***.

B: Use division to convert to a ***decimal***.

Label the place values in your answer.

C. To convert a **percentage** to a **decimal**, move the

decimal point _____ _____ to the

_____, _____ from the percent symbol.

D. To convert a **decimal** to a **percentage**, move the

decimal point _____ _____ to the

_____, _____ where the % symbol goes.

E. Convert the percentages below to decimals.

Percentage	Decimal
2%	
20%	
34%	
15%	
1%	
9%	
8%	
10%	
72%	
253%	★

Percentage	Decimal
60%	
6%	
45.2%	★
90%	
63%	
100%	★
8.15%	★
40%	
4%	
80%	

F. Convert the decimals below to percentages.

Decimal	Percentage
0.53	
0.02	
0.2	
0.18	
0.80	
0.20	
1.53	★
1	
0.4	
0.8	

Decimal	Percentage
0.7	
0.04	
0.59	
0.3	
0.08	
0.049	★
0.07	
0.035	★
2.46	★
0.625	★

Lesson 4: Converting Fractions, Decimals and Percentages

Fraction
Decimal ⟷ Percentage

Part 1: Use **proportions** to convert fractions to percentages and decimals.

Fraction/Proportion	Percentage	Decimal
A. $\dfrac{41}{50}$		
B. $\dfrac{7}{10}$		
C. $\dfrac{3}{50}$		
D. $\dfrac{1}{2}$		
E. $\dfrac{1}{50}$		

Fraction/Proportion	Percentage	Decimal
F. $\dfrac{3}{5}$		
G. $\dfrac{3}{4}$		
H. $\dfrac{3}{25}$		
I. $\dfrac{20}{25}$		
J. $\dfrac{1}{20}$		

Part 2: Use **division** to convert fractions to decimals and percentages.

Fraction to Decimal	Percentage
K. $\dfrac{1}{8}$	
L. $\dfrac{2}{8}$	
M. $\dfrac{3}{8}$	

Fraction to Decimal	Percentage
N. Use division. $\dfrac{3}{6}$	
O. Simplify first, then use division. $\dfrac{3}{6}$	
P. Simplify first, then use a <u>proportion.</u> $\dfrac{3}{6}$	

Lesson 5: Converting Decimals and Percentages to Fractions

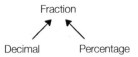

Fraction

Decimal   Percentage

Part 1: Factor.

100

____ · ____

____ · ____

____ · ____

____ · ____

____ · ____

Part 2: Follow along with your instructor to review the divisibility rules.

Divisor	Divisibility Rule
2	ends in _____, _____, _____, _____, or _____
4	
5	ends in _____ or _____
10	ends in _____
20	ends in _____, _____, _____, _____, or _____
25	ends in _____, _____, _____, or _____ (Think 25¢, 50¢, 75¢, $1.00)
50	ends in _____ or _____
100	ends in _____

Part 3: Convert percentages and decimals to fractions, then **simplify**. (If you get stuck working with large numbers, see if you can divide by 10 to make the numbers more manageable.)

	Percentage	Fraction
A.	50%	
B.	25%	
C.	80%	
D.	70%	
E.	75%	
F.	55%	
G.	20%	
H.	16.1%	★

	Decimal	Fraction
I.	0.06	
J.	0.6	
K.	0.24	
L.	0.2	
M.	0.08	
N.	0.8	
O.	0.5	
P.	0.501	★

Name_____

Fraction

Decimal ⟶ Percentage

Lesson 6: Batting Averages

Directions: Follow along with your instructor to complete this lesson.

In baseball, an **"at bat"** is when it's a player's turn to bat against a pitcher. A player earns a **"hit"** when he or she hits a fair ball and reaches at least first base safely. ("Walks" don't count as "at bats," and "errors" don't count as "hits.")

The **batting average** is the number of hits divided by the number of at bats. Batting averages are usually written to three decimal places (the thousandths place value) but pronounced without saying "thousandths."

Greg, Hannah, Iris, Javier, Kevin, and Larry play on a baseball team. So far, they have the statistics shown below.

	Greg	Hannah	Iris	Javier	Kevin	Larry
Hits	2	4	3	1	2	3
At Bats	7	9	5	4	9	8
A. Write the batting average as a fraction.						
B.	With your partner, decide which player has the highest batting average. Defend your answer.					
C. Convert the batting averages from fractions to decimals (round to three decimal places).						
D.	Who had the highest batting average? _____ Who had the lowest batting average? _____ These batting averages were easier to compare as _____ instead of as _____.					
E. Convert the batting averages to percentages (to one decimal place).						

Lesson 7: All Conversions

Fraction

Decimal ←→ Percentage

Directions: Convert between fractions, decimals, and percentages.

Convert using proportions.

Convert using division.

Part 1:

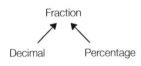

Fraction

Decimal   Percentage

Fraction	Percentage	Decimal
A. $\frac{33}{50}$		
B. $\frac{3}{10}$		
C. $\frac{1}{25}$		
D. $\frac{3}{4}$		
E. $\frac{7}{20}$		

Fraction to Decimal	Percentage
F. $\frac{1}{8}$	
G. $\frac{3}{8}$	

Part 2:

Fraction

Decimal   Percentage

Decimal	Fraction (Simplify)
H. 0.04	
I. 0.4	
J. 0.18	
K. 0.12	
L. 0.6	

Percentage	Fraction (Simplify)
M. 60%	
N. 53%	
O. 50%	
P. 12%	
Q. 25%	

Part 3:

Fraction

Decimal ←→ Percentage

Percentage	Decimal
R. 3%	
S. 30%	
T. 49%	
U. 100%	
V. 1%	
W. 80%	
X. 8%	

Decimal	Percentage
Y. 0.73	
Z. 0.009	
AA. 0.9	
AB. 0.54	
AC. 0.5	
AD. 0.005	
AE. 1.49	

Lesson 8: All Conversions

Directions: Convert between fractions, decimals, and percentages.

Convert using proportions.

Convert using division.

Part 1:

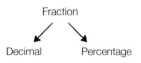

	Fraction	Percentage	Decimal
A.	$\frac{41}{50}$		
B.	$\frac{7}{10}$		
C.	$\frac{2}{25}$		
D.	$\frac{1}{4}$		
E.	$\frac{1}{20}$		

Fraction to Decimal	Percentage
F. $\frac{5}{8}$	
G. $\frac{7}{8}$	

Part 2:

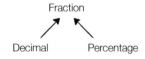

	Decimal	Fraction (Simplify)
H.	0.06	
I.	0.6	
J.	0.14	
K.	0.16	
L.	0.4	

	Percentage	Fraction (Simplify)
M.	50%	
N.	23%	
O.	80%	
P.	70%	
Q.	75%	

Part 3:

Fraction

Decimal ⟷ Percentage

	Percentage	Decimal
R.	4%	
S.	40%	
T.	37%	
U.	100%	
V.	1%	
W.	90%	
X.	9%	

	Decimal	Percentage
Y.	0.57	
Z.	0.02	
AA.	0.2	
AB.	0.16	
AC.	0.8	
AD.	0.08	
AE.	1.53	

Name_____

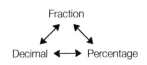

Lesson 9: The Power to Choose

Part 1: Convert percentages to decimals and fractions.

Percentage	Decimal	Fraction (Simplify)
A. 25%		
B. 50%		
C. 75%		

Part 2: Solve. Complete all of Column 1 first, then complete all of Column 2.

	Column 1 Solve using decimals.	Column 2 Solve using fractions.
Find 20% of 25.	D.	H.
Find 50% of 18.	E.	I.
Find 25% of 16.	F.	J.
Find 75% of 32.	G.	K.

The ability to _____ gives you the _____ _____ _____ the easiest method.

Applications Involving Conversions:

Markups & Markdowns

Go down your **Success Tracker** in the order shown below and write your score for each of the activities as you complete them. The goal is to make any corrections necessary to earn a score of 100%.

Lesson	Lesson Name	Score
KEY LESSON ⊶ A	Computational Efficiency	
B	Simplifying Subtraction with Zeroes	
C	Trailing Zeroes	
D	Trailing Zeroes	
E	Trailing Zeroes	
F	Calculating 15% Easily Without Multiplying	
G	Hanging Zeroes	
KEY LESSON ⊶ 10	Markups vs. Markdowns (Discounts)	
11	Tax and Tip (Markups)	
KEY LESSON ⊶ 12	Review of Key Conversions	
13	Single Markup Problems	
14	Single Markdown (Discount) Problems	
15	One-Year Simple Interest (Markups)	
16	Multiple Markups	
17	Multiple Markdowns	
18	Markdowns Followed by Markups	
19	Simple vs. Compound Interest	
20	Simple vs. Compound Interest	

Making Sense of Conversions | © ironboxeducation.com | **Teachers: Log in for demo videos.**

Name_____

Efficiency Lesson A: Computational Efficiency

Introduction: In the upcoming lessons, we are going to work with word problems that involve conversions between percentages, decimals, and fractions.

As with any type of math, it will definitely help if you are both fast and accurate because it will save you time, and it will prevent unnecessary mistakes.

In the next series of lessons, you will learn strategies to solve problems quickly and easily.

Example 1: Look at the two students below who were given the same problem:

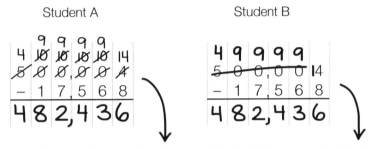

Student A solved the problem in **_16 steps,_** but Student B only needed **_8 steps._**

How many steps did Student B save?_____

Example 2: Student A and Student B were asked, "What is 20% of $410.00?"

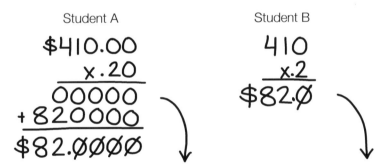

Student A solved the problem in **_17 steps,_** but Student B only needed **_3 steps._**

How many steps did Student B save?_____

By using these strategies, math will become much easier and enjoyable for you (and you will finish your work **_much faster_**).

Efficiency Lesson B: The Simple Way to Subtract with Zeroes

Part 1: Follow along with you instructor to solve the two subtraction problems below using Method 1 (standard regrouping) and Method 2 (shortcut for regrouping when subtracting with zeroes).

Method 1

Method 2

```
  5 0 0,0 0 4          5 0 0,0 0 4
-   1 7,5 6 8        -   1 7,5 6 8
```

Part 2: Solve using the shortcut for regrouping when subtracting with zeroes. Be sure to use your pencil tip to **"touch and protect"** the number that you are subtracting from so that you don't accidentally cross it out.

Careful! Touch and protect the 0
in the ones place value so you
don't cross it out accidentally.

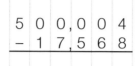

```
  6 0 0,0 4 9          8 0 0,0 0 0          4 7 9,0 0 9          6 2 0,0 0 0
-   1 7,5 6 8        -   1 7,5 6 8        -   1 7,5 6 8        -   1 7,5 6 8
```

Part 3: Subtract. When regrouping, be sure you write a number above every place value that you cross out. For example, when you cross out three digits in "100" in the first problem, replace those three digits with "099" instead of just "99" (which has only two digits).

```
  3 5 1,0 0 0          7 0 1,0 0 3          2 1 0,0 0 0          4 0 1,0 0 0
-   1 7,5 6 8        -   1 7,5 6 8        -   1 7,5 6 8        -   1 7,5 6 8
```

Part 4: Subtract.

```
  6 0 0,3 0 0          1 0 1,0 0 9          8 0 7,0 0 0          4 1 5,2 0 9
-   1 7,5 6 8        -   1 7,5 6 8        -   1 7,5 6 8        -   1 7,5 6 8
```

Efficiency Lesson C: Trailing Zeroes

When adding or subtracting decimals, the decimal points must line up so that the place values line up. But why?

Think back to the Apples Plus Apples lesson in *Making Sense of Fractions.* Thirds can only be added with thirds, just like apples can only be added with apples. It does not make sense to add things with different names such as pencils and cars.

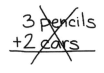

```
 1 third          1 apple          3 pencils
+1 third         +1 apple         +2 cars
 2 thirds         2 apples
```

The same logic applies when working with place value. The billions place value can only be added with the billions place value, the hundredths place value can only be added with the hundredths place value, and so on.

```
 4 billion          3 hundredths
+1 billion         +2 hundredths
 5 billion          5 hundredths
```

When adding or subtracting decimals, the place values have to line up. The best way to make sure the place values line up is to make sure the decimal points line up.

To make it easier to line up the decimal points when adding decimals, use trailing zeroes so that each addend has the same number of digits after the decimal point.

Part 1: When **adding or subtracting decimals,** use trailing zeroes as necessary so that each number has the same number of digits after the decimal point. Rewrite each problem in the working space, then solve. Write your final answer without trailing zeroes.

5.00 + 2.231

= _____

5.00 – 2.231

= _____

Part 2: When **multiplying decimals,** you do not need to line up the decimal points (since you're not adding or subtracting). So, should we keep trailing zeroes or should we omit them?

Solve each problem using the two methods below to find out. Remember to write your decimal point in your product correctly (if the two factors had five decimal places combined, you product should have five decimal places as well). Write your final answer without trailing zeroes.

Method 1
Keep trailing zeroes when multiplying decimals.

5.00 x 2.231

= _____

Method 2
Omit trailing zeroes when multiplying decimals.

5.00 x 2.231

= _____

In order to save _____ and reduce

_____, we should _____ trailing

zeroes when multiplying decimals.

Efficiency Lesson D: Trailing Zeroes

Directions: Each problem in each row uses the same two numbers. Use the working space to add, subtract, or multiply as indicated. Use or omit trailing zeroes appropriately. Final answers should have no trailing zeroes.

Row A   6.0 x 3.14   6.0 + 3.14   6.0 − 3.14

= _____   = _____   = _____

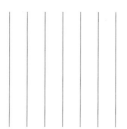

Row B   12 − 0.15   12 + 0.15   12 x 0.15

= _____   = _____   = _____

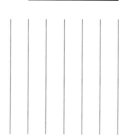
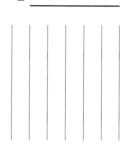

Row C   8.00 + 2.345   8.00 x 2.345   8.00 − 2.345

= _____   = _____   = _____

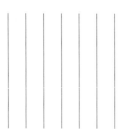
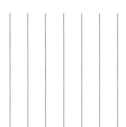
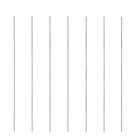

Row D   6.3 − 4   6.3 + 4   6.3 x 4

= _____   = _____   = _____

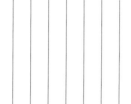
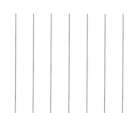
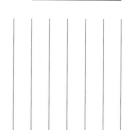

Efficiency Lesson E: Trailing Zeroes

Directions: Each problem in each row uses the same two numbers. Use the working space to add, subtract, or multiply as indicated. Use or omit trailing zeroes appropriately. Final answers should have no trailing zeroes.

Row A   5.0   x   3.14   5.0   +   3.14   5.0   –   3.14

= _____   = _____   = _____

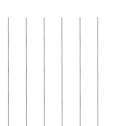
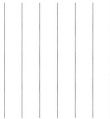

Row B   18   –   0.20   18   +   0.20   18   x   0.20

= _____   = _____   = _____

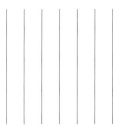

Row C   9.0   +   8.83   9.0   x   8.83   9.0   –   8.83

= _____   = _____   = _____

Row D   23.00   –   0.15   23.00   +   0.15   23.00   x   0.15

= _____   = _____   = _____

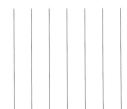
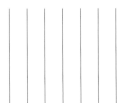
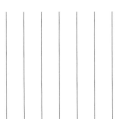

Efficiency Lesson F: Calculating 15% Easily Without Multiplying

Part A: The value 15% is a useful percentage in real life. For example, it's often used for calculating tip at a restaurant. However, calculating 15% by multiplying involves a lot of steps, as you'll see below.

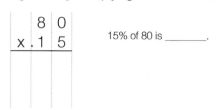

15% of 80 is _____.

Part B: Since calculating 15% by multiplying involves a lot of work, let's break it up (decompose it) into two easier steps that you'll frequently be able to do in your head.

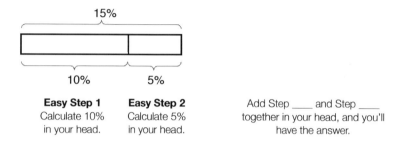

Easy Step 1	**Easy Step 2**	Add Step ____ and Step ____
Calculate 10%	Calculate 5%	together in your head, and you'll
in your head.	in your head.	have the answer.

Part C: Calculating 10% of a number is easy to do in your head. Too find out how, calculate 10% of 80 using multiplication. Then, figure out how to get the answer in your head without multiplying.

$$\begin{array}{r} 8\ 0 \\ \times\ .1 \\ \hline \end{array}$$

10% of 80 is _____.

How do you find 10% of 80 without multiplying?

Move the decimal point one space to the _____.

Part D: To find 15% of a number without multiplying, follow these steps:

- Find 10% of the number.
- Find 5% of the number **(5% is half of 10%).**
- Add the 10% part with the 5% part to get 15%.

Without multiplying, find the answer to our original problem in Part A. Remember, **5% is half of 10%.**

15% of 80 = _____	
10% ⟶	Your final answer from **Part A** was _____.
+5% ⟶	Your final answer from **Part D** was also _____, but notice how you could do the calculations in your head.
15% ⟶	

Now try these other easy examples below, and notice how you can do the calculations in your head.

15% of 500 = _____	15% of 120 = _____	15% of 4,000 = _____	15% of 20,000 = _____
10% ⟶	10% ⟶	10% ⟶	10% ⟶
+5% ⟶	+5% ⟶	+5% ⟶	+5% ⟶
15% ⟶	15% ⟶	15% ⟶	15% ⟶

Efficiency Lesson G: Hanging Zeroes

Part 1: Follow along with you instructor to solve the multiplication problem below using Methods 1, 2, and 3.

Method 1　　　　　Method 2　　　　　Method 3

```
    6  0  0
  x    5  0
  _____
```

Part 2: Solve using the Hanging Zeroes shortcut.

A. 4 x 600	B. 300 x 5	C. 500 x 200	D. 4 x 5,000
		Be careful!	Be careful!
E. 34 x 1,000	F. 200 x 2,500	G. 26 x 800	H. 18,000 x 20
I. 60 x 60	J. 60 x 60 x 3	K. 5 x 60 x 60	L. 24 x 60 x 60

Part 3: Multiply by powers of 10.

M. 600 x 100	N. 34 x 1,000	O. 270 x 10,000	P. 25 x 100,000

Making Sense of Conversions | © ironboxeducation.com | **Teachers: Log in for demo videos.**

Name_____

Lesson 10: Markups vs. Markdowns (Discounts)

Directions: Follow along with your instructor to complete this lesson.

Markups	Markdowns (Discounts)
1. A $200.00 dress is marked up by 30%.	2. A $200.00 dress is marked down by 30%.

Bar Model	Calculations	Bar Model	Calculations
100%		100%	

Original Price:

Markup/Markdown:

Final Price:

Original Price:

Markup/Markdown:

Final Price:

Markups	Markdowns (Discounts)
1.	1.
2.	2.
3.	3.
4.	4.
5.	5.
6.	6.

Lesson 11: Tax and Tip (Markups)

Directions: Solve and visually depict the information accurately using bar models. Quantify each element of the bar model, including the sum. ***Avoid trailing zeroes when multiplying.***

1. Dinner costs $68.00. Tax is 10%, and tip is 20% of the base.

Base: _____

Tax: _____

Tip: _____

Total: _____

Bar Model	Tax	Tip
100%		

Use the correct number of trailing zeroes for currency.

2. You give a 15% tip for a $120.00 meal (remember Efficiency Lesson F). Tax is 8%.

Base: _____

Tax: _____

Tip: _____

Total: _____

Bar Model	Tax	Tip
100%		

Use the correct number of trailing zeroes for currency.

3. Tax is 9%. The base amount is $40.00, and you leave an 18% tip. (HINT: 18% is double of 9%.)

Base: _____

Tax: _____

Tip: _____

Total: _____

	Tax	Tip
Solve by *visualizing* the bar model in your head instead of drawing it on paper.		

4. You leave a 20% tip for a $32.00 meal in a city with a 5% tax rate.

Base: _____

Tax: _____

Tip: _____

Total: _____

	Tax	Tip
Solve by *visualizing* the bar model in your head instead of drawing it on paper.		

Lesson 12: Review of Key Conversions

Part 1: Factor.

```
100
      ____  .  ____

      ____  .  ____

      ____  .  ____

      ____  .  ____

      ____  .  ____
```

Part 2: Convert.

Percentage	Decimal	Fraction (Simplify)
25%	A.	B.
50%	C.	D.
75%	E.	F.
100%	G.	H.

Part 3: Solve using decimals. Then, solve the same problem using fractions.

	Decimal	Fraction (Simplify)
Calculate 25% of 36.	I.	J.
Calculate 75% of 28.	K.	L.

Lesson 13: Single Markup Problems

Directions: Solve and visually depict the information accurately using bar models. Quantify each element of the bar model, including the sum. ***Avoid trailing zeroes when multiplying.***

1. A $600.00 suit is marked up by 50%. (HINT: Convert 50% to a fraction instead of a decimal.)

Original Price: _____

Markup/Markdown: _____

Selling Price: _____

Bar Model	Calculations
100%	

2. A furniture store applies a 25% markup to a $280.00 media console. (HINT: Use a fraction instead of a decimal.)

Original Price: _____

Markup/Markdown: _____

Selling Price: _____

Bar Model	Calculations
100%	

3. A $413.00 bookshelf is marked up by 30%.

Original Price: _____

Markup/Markdown: _____

Selling Price: _____

	Calculations
Solve by ***visualizing*** the bar model in your head instead of drawing it on paper.	

4. A retailer marks up a $923.00 rug by 7%.

Original Price: _____

Markup/Markdown: _____

Selling Price: _____

	Calculations
Solve by ***visualizing*** the bar model in your head instead of drawing it on paper.	

Lesson 14: Single Markdown (Discount) Problems

Directions: Solve and visually depict the information accurately using bar models. Quantify each element of the bar model, including the sum. ***Avoid trailing zeroes when multiplying.***

1. A rug is marked down 40% from its original price of $900.00.

Original Price: _____

Markup/Markdown: _____

Selling Price: _____

Bar Model	Calculations
100%	

2. A $600.00 suit is marked down by 15%. (HINT: Remember Efficiency Lesson F.)

Original Price: _____

Markup/Markdown: _____

Selling Price: _____

Bar Model	Calculations
100%	

3. A 25% off sale is held for a $280.00 media console.

Original Price: _____

Markup/Markdown: _____

Selling Price: _____

	Calculations
Solve by ***visualizing*** the bar model in your head instead of drawing it on paper.	

4. A $4,000.00 computer is discounted 15%.

Original Price: _____

Markup/Markdown: _____

Selling Price: _____

	Calculations
Solve by ***visualizing*** the bar model in your head instead of drawing it on paper.	

Lesson 15: One-Year Simple Interest (Markups)

Directions: Solve and visually depict the information accurately using bar models. Quantify each element of the bar model, including the sum. ***Avoid trailing zeroes when multiplying.***

1. $300.00 principal, 10% simple interest per year

Principal: _____

Interest Year 1: _____

Balance Year 1: _____

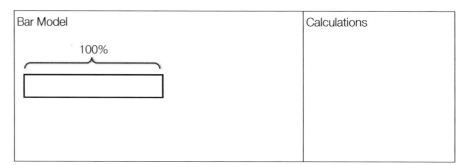

2. $200.00 principal, 6% simple interest per year

Principal: _____

Interest Year 1: _____

Balance Year 1: _____

3. $500.00 principal, 20% simple interest per year

Principal: _____

Interest Year 1: _____

Balance Year 1: _____

	Calculations
Solve by ***visualizing*** the bar model in your head instead of drawing it on paper.	

4. $800.00 principal, 8% simple interest per year

Principal: _____

Interest Year 1: _____

Balance Year 1: _____

	Calculations
Solve by ***visualizing*** the bar model in your head instead of drawing it on paper.	

Name_____

Lesson 16: Multiple Markups

Directions: Solve and visually depict the information accurately using bar models. Quantify each element of the bar model, including the sum. ***Avoid trailing zeroes when multiplying.***

1. A $280.00 media console is marked up by 25%, then marked up again by an additional 10%.

Original Price: _____

Markup/Markdown 1: _____

Selling Price 1: _____

Markup/Markdown 2: _____

Selling Price 2: _____

Markup #1 100%	Calculations
Markup #2	Calculations

2. A $600.00 suit is marked up 50%, then marked up again by 25%.

Original Price: _____

Markup/Markdown 1: _____

Selling Price 1: _____

Markup/Markdown 2: _____

Selling Price 2: _____

Markup #1 100%	Calculations
Markup #2	Calculations

3. A home improvement store marks up a $750.00 cabinet by 60%, then marks it up another 20%.

Original Price: _____

Markup/Markdown 1: _____

Selling Price 1: _____

Markup/Markdown 2: _____

Selling Price 2: _____

	Calculations
Solve by ***visualizing*** the bar model in your head instead of drawing it on paper.	
Solve by ***visualizing*** the bar model in your head instead of drawing it on paper.	Calculations

Lesson 17: Multiple Markdowns

Directions: Solve and visually depict the information accurately using bar models. Quantify each element of the bar model, including the sum. ***Avoid trailing zeroes when multiplying.***

1. A dining table is marked down 40% from its original price of $360.00, then marked down another 20%.

Original Price: _____

Markup/Markdown 1: _____

Selling Price 1: _____

Markup/Markdown 2: _____

Selling Price 2: _____

Markdown #1 100%	Calculations
Markdown #2	Calculations

2. A $280.00 media console goes on sale of 25% off, then gets marked down an additional 20%.

Original Price: _____

Markup/Markdown 1: _____

Selling Price 1: _____

Markup/Markdown 2: _____

Selling Price 2: _____

Markdown #1 100%	Calculations
Markdown #2	Calculations

3. A $600.00 suit is discounted by 50%, then goes on sale for an additional 25% off.

Original Price: _____

Markup/Markdown 1: _____

Selling Price 1: _____

Markup/Markdown 2: _____

Selling Price 2: _____

	Calculations
Solve by ***visualizing*** the bar model in your head instead of drawing it on paper.	Calculations
Solve by ***visualizing*** the bar model in your head instead of drawing it on paper.	

Lesson 18: Markdowns Followed by Markups

Directions: Solve and visually depict the information accurately using bar models. Quantify each element of the bar model, including the sum. **_Avoid trailing zeroes when multiplying._**

1. A $750.00 cabinet goes on sale for 60% off. A customer purchases it and pays 10% tax.

Original Price: _____

Markup/Markdown: _____

Selling Price: _____

Tax: _____

Final Cost: _____

Markdown	Calculations
100%	
Markup	Calculations

2. A $28.00 shirt is discounted by 25%. A customer purchases it and pays 5% tax.

Original Price: _____

Markup/Markdown: _____

Selling Price: _____

Tax: _____

Final Cost: _____

Markdown	Calculations
100%	
Markup	Calculations

3. A $30.00 shirt is discounted by 40%. A customer purchases it and pays 9% tax.

Original Price: _____

Markup/Markdown: _____

Selling Price: _____

Tax: _____

Final Cost: _____

	Calculations
Solve by **_visualizing_** the bar model in your head instead of drawing it on paper.	
Solve by **_visualizing_** the bar model in your head instead of drawing it on paper.	Calculations

Lesson 19: Simple vs. Compound Interest

Directions: Solve and visually depict the information accurately using bar models. Quantify each element of the bar model, including the sum. *Avoid trailing zeroes when multiplying.*

$300.00 principal, 10% interest per year for 2 years.

SIMPLE INTEREST

Interest earned is always kept separate from the original principal. This means that the principal stays the same from year to year, and the interest earned each year stays the same as well.

Principal: _____

Interest Year 1: _____

Balance Year 1: _____

Interest Year 2: _____

Balance Year 2: _____

Years 1 & 2 100%	Calculations

Follow along with your instructor to learn the shortcut for finding the Year 2 simple interest balance.

COMPOUND INTEREST

Interest earned gets added to the principal. This means that the principal is allowed to grow larger and larger each year. Since the principal keeps getting larger and larger each year, the interest earned each year gets larger and larger as well.

Principal: _____

Interest Year 1: _____

Balance Year 1: _____

Interest Year 2: _____

Balance Year 2: _____

Year 1 100%	Calculations
Year 2	Calculations

Check the Year 1 balance and the Year 2 balance with your instructor.

If you were earning interest, would you rather have simple interest or compound interest?_____

Lesson 20: Simple vs. Compound Interest

Directions: Solve and visually depict the information accurately using bar models. Quantify each element of the bar model, including the sum. ***Avoid trailing zeroes when multiplying.***

$500 principal, 20% interest per year for 3 years.

SIMPLE INTEREST

Interest earned is always kept separate from the original principal. This means that the principal stays the same from year to year, and the interest earned each year stays the same as well.

Principal: _____

Interest Year 1: _____

Balance Year 1: _____

Interest Year 2: _____

Balance Year 2: _____

Interest Year 3: _____

Balance Year 3: _____

Years 1, 2, and 3 100%	Calculations

Follow along with your instructor to learn the shortcut for finding the Year 3 simple interest balance.

COMPOUND INTEREST

Interest earned gets added to the principal. This means that the principal is allowed to grow larger and larger each year. Since the principal keeps getting larger and larger each year, the interest earned each year gets larger and larger as well.

Principal: _____

Interest Year 1: _____

Balance Year 1: _____

Interest Year 2: _____

Balance Year 2: _____

Interest Year 3: _____

Balance Year 3: _____

Check the balance for Years 1, 2, and 3.

Year 1 100%	Calculations
Year 2	Calculations
Year 3	Calculations

Making Sense of Conversions | © ironboxeducation.com | **Teachers: Log in for demo videos.**

Answer Keys and Correcting Student Work

The answer keys in this section are fully annotated. They show not only the correct answer, but how to get there. This makes is easier to troubleshoot student errors so they can correct them.

Provide immediate feedback so that students know how they are doing. Take a look at the sample work below.

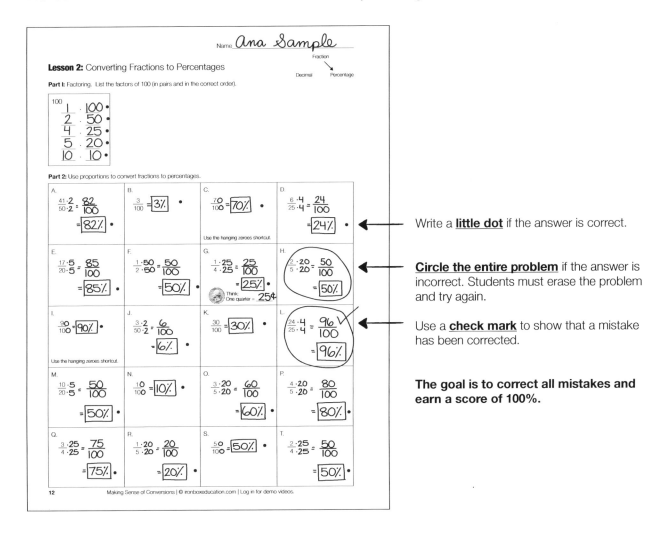

Write a **little dot** if the answer is correct.

Circle the entire problem if the answer is incorrect. Students must erase the problem and try again.

Use a **check mark** to show that a mistake has been corrected.

The goal is to correct all mistakes and earn a score of 100%.

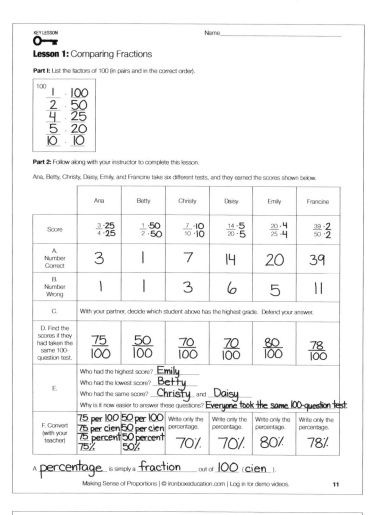

KEY LESSON

Name_____

Lesson 1: Comparing Fractions

Part I: List the factors of 100 (in pairs and in the correct order).

```
100 |  1 · 100
     |  2 · 50
     |  4 · 25
     |  5 · 20
     | 10 · 10
```

Part 2: Follow along with your instructor to complete this lesson.

Ana, Betty, Christy, Daisy, Emily, and Francine take six different tests, and they earned the scores shown below.

	Ana	Betty	Christy	Daisy	Emily	Francine
Score	$\frac{3 \cdot 25}{4 \cdot 25}$	$\frac{1 \cdot 50}{2 \cdot 50}$	$\frac{7 \cdot 10}{10 \cdot 10}$	$\frac{14 \cdot 5}{20 \cdot 5}$	$\frac{20 \cdot 4}{25 \cdot 4}$	$\frac{39 \cdot 2}{50 \cdot 2}$
A. Number Correct	3	1	7	14	20	39
B. Number Wrong	1	1	3	6	5	11
C.	With your partner, decide which student above has the highest grade. Defend your answer.					
D. Find the scores if they had taken the same 100-question test.	$\frac{75}{100}$	$\frac{50}{100}$	$\frac{70}{100}$	$\frac{70}{100}$	$\frac{80}{100}$	$\frac{78}{100}$
E.	Who had the highest score? Emily Who had the lowest score? Betty Who had the same score? Christy and Daisy Why is it now easier to answer these questions? Everyone took the same 100-question test.					
F. Convert (with your teacher)	75 per 100 75 per cien 75 percent 75%	50 per 100 50 per cien 50 percent 50%	Write only the percentage. 70%	Write only the percentage. 70%	Write only the percentage. 80%	Write only the percentage. 78%

A **percentage** is simply a **fraction** out of **100** (cien).

Making Sense of Proportions | © ironboxeducation.com | Log in for demo videos.   11

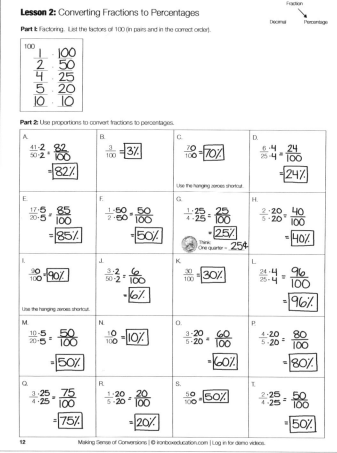

Name_____

Lesson 2: Converting Fractions to Percentages

Fraction
Decimal → Percentage

Part I: Factoring. List the factors of 100 (in pairs and in the correct order).

```
100 |  1 · 100
     |  2 · 50
     |  4 · 25
     |  5 · 20
     | 10 · 10
```

Part 2: Use proportions to convert fractions to percentages.

A. $\frac{41 \cdot 2}{50 \cdot 2} = \frac{82}{100}$ = 82%

B. $\frac{3}{100}$ = 3%

C. $\frac{7}{10} \to \frac{70}{100}$ = 70% Use the hanging zeroes shortcut.

D. $\frac{6 \cdot 4}{25 \cdot 4} = \frac{24}{100}$ = 24%

E. $\frac{17 \cdot 5}{20 \cdot 5} = \frac{85}{100}$ = 85%

F. $\frac{1 \cdot 50}{2 \cdot 50} = \frac{50}{100}$ = 50%

G. $\frac{1 \cdot 25}{4 \cdot 25} = \frac{25}{100}$ = 25% Think: One quarter = 25¢

H. $\frac{2 \cdot 20}{5 \cdot 20} = \frac{40}{100}$ = 40%

I. $\frac{90}{100}$ = 90%

J. $\frac{3 \cdot 2}{50 \cdot 2} = \frac{6}{100}$ = 6% Use the hanging zeroes shortcut.

K. $\frac{30}{100}$ = 30%

L. $\frac{24 \cdot 4}{25 \cdot 4} = \frac{96}{100}$ = 96%

M. $\frac{10 \cdot 5}{20 \cdot 5} = \frac{50}{100}$ = 50%

N. $\frac{10}{100}$ = 10%

O. $\frac{3 \cdot 20}{5 \cdot 20} = \frac{60}{100}$ = 60%

P. $\frac{4 \cdot 20}{5 \cdot 20} = \frac{80}{100}$ = 80%

Q. $\frac{3 \cdot 25}{4 \cdot 25} = \frac{75}{100}$ = 75%

R. $\frac{1 \cdot 20}{5 \cdot 20} = \frac{20}{100}$ = 20%

S. $\frac{50}{100}$ = 50%

T. $\frac{2 \cdot 25}{4 \cdot 25} = \frac{50}{100}$ = 50%

12   Making Sense of Conversions | © ironboxeducation.com | Log in for demo videos.

Key Points from Demo Video – Lesson 1
Comparing Fractions

This is the most important lesson in the unit because it shows students why conversions matter.

In Part 1, students review the factors of 100. They will use these factors of 100 in Part 2.

Part 2 explains that Ana, Betty, Christy, Daisy, Emily, and Francine each take six different tests. In Parts A and B, students write the number of problems that each person got correct or wrong. In Part C, based on this information, students must decide who has the highest grade.

This is a difficult and confusing decision to make because all six students took different tests. It's difficult to compare the results in the form given (fractions with unlike denominators).

In Part D, students use proportions to find each persons' score if they had taken the same 100-question test. In Part E, students see that the comparison is much easier to make now that everyone is taking the same test.

In Part F, students learn to logically and easily convert fractions out of 100 into percentages.

Key Points from Demo Video – Lesson 2
Converting Fractions to Percentages

Lesson 2 builds upon Lesson 1. Students use proportions and factors of 100 to easily convert fractions to percentages.

In Part 1, students review the factors of 100, which they will use in Part 2.

In Part 2, all the fractions shown have a denominator that is a factor of 100. Students use proportions to convert each fraction to an equivalent fraction out of 100.

Fractions out of 100 are easy to convert to percentages because "percent" means "per 100." In the previous lesson, students learned that "100" in Spanish is "cien." Therefore, "per 100" means "per cien," which means "percent." A percentage is simply a fraction out of 100 (cien).

In Box A, 41/50 is equal to 82/100, which is 82%.

Box B shows 3/100, which is already a fraction out of 100, so no conversion is needed.

In Box C, 7/10 can be converted to 7/100 simply by adding hanging zeroes.

Key Points from Demo Video – Lesson 3
Converting Fractions, Decimals, and Percentages

Lesson 3 makes logical connections between fractions, decimals, and percentages so that they can be easily converted from one form to another.

Part 1 provides a place value review that will be used in Part 2.

In Part 2, the fraction 1/4 is converted into both a percentage and a decimal.

First, the fraction 1/4 is converted into a percentage using a proportion. *A proportion can be used to make this conversion because the denominator of 4 is a factor of 100.*

Next, the fraction 1/4 is converted into a decimal using long division. The place value names in the quotient of .25 are labeled as 10th and 100ths.

This exercise helps students make the connection that the percentage of 25% (or 25 per 100) is equivalent to the decimal 0.25, which is pronounced as "25 hundredths."

In Parts C and D, students practice converting from percentages to decimals and vice versa.

Key Points from Demo Video – Lesson 4
Converting Fractions, Decimals, and Percentages

In Lesson 4, students use different methods to convert fractions to decimals and percentages.

In Part 1, students convert by using proportions. *Proportions can be used for these problems because each of the fractions have a denominator that is a factor of 100.* The denominators used are 2, 4, 5, 10, 20, 25, and 50.

In Part 2, students convert by using long division. Proportions can't be used to make these conversions because the denominators of the fractions (8 and 6) are not factors of 100. This is why they must use long division for these problems, as they did in problem B of the the previous lesson.

The fraction 1/8 converts to 12.5%, and the fraction 3/8 converts to 37.5%. Notice that of these answers have a decimal within the percentage.

The last section of Part 2 shows the fraction 3/6 being converted to a percentage using three methods – 1) use long division, 2) simplify first, then use long division, 3) simplify first, then use a proportion. *This shows that there are multiple ways to perform a conversion.*

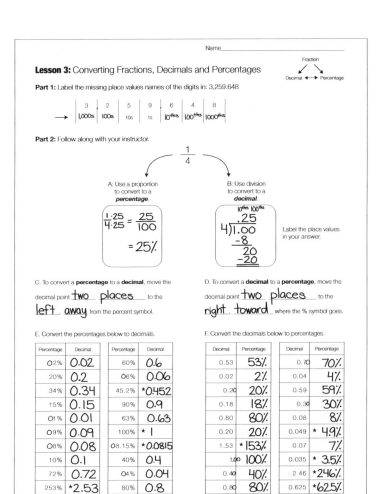

Lesson 3: Converting Fractions, Decimals and Percentages

Fraction
Decimal ←→ Percentage

Part 1: Label the missing place values names of the digits in: 3,259.648

3	2	5	9	6	4	8
1,000s	100s	10s	1s	10ths	100ths	1000ths

Part 2: Follow along with your instructor.

$\frac{1}{4}$

A: Use a proportion to convert to a **percentage**.

$\frac{1\cdot25}{4\cdot25} = \frac{25}{100}$

$= 25\%$

B: Use division to convert to a **decimal**.

10ths 100ths
.25
4)1.00
−8
20
−20

Label the place values in your answer.

C. To convert a **percentage** to a **decimal**, move the decimal point two places to the left, away from the percent symbol.

D. To convert a **decimal** to a **percentage**, move the decimal point two places to the right, toward where the % symbol goes.

E. Convert the percentages below to decimals.

Percentage	Decimal	Percentage	Decimal
02%	0.02	60%	0.6
20%	0.2	06%	0.06
34%	0.34	45.2%	*0.452
15%	0.15	90%	0.9
01%	0.01	63%	0.63
09%	0.09	100%	* 1
08%	0.08	08.15%	*0.0815
10%	0.1	40%	0.4
72%	0.72	04%	0.04
253%	*2.53	80%	0.8

F. Convert the decimals below to percentages.

Decimal	Percentage	Decimal	Percentage
0.53	53%	0.70	70%
0.02	2%	0.04	4%
0.20	20%	0.59	59%
0.18	18%	0.30	30%
0.80	80%	0.08	8%
0.20	20%	0.049	* 4.9%
1.53	*153%	0.07	7%
1.00	100%	0.035	* 3.5%
0.40	40%	2.46	*246%
0.80	80%	0.625	*62.5%

Making Sense of Conversions | © ironboxeducation.com | Log in for demo videos.   13

Lesson 4: Converting Fractions, Decimals and Percentages

Fraction
Decimal ←→ Percentage

Part 1: Use **proportions** to convert fractions to percentages and decimals.

Fraction/Proportion	Percentage	Decimal	Fraction/Proportion	Percentage	Decimal
A. $\frac{41\cdot2}{50\cdot2} = \frac{82}{100}$	82%	0.82	F. $\frac{3\cdot20}{5\cdot20} = \frac{60}{100}$	60%	0.6
B. $\frac{70}{100}$	70%	0.7	G. $\frac{3\cdot25}{4\cdot25} = \frac{75}{100}$	75%	0.75
C. $\frac{3\cdot2}{50\cdot2} = \frac{6}{100}$	6%	0.06	H. $\frac{3\cdot4}{25\cdot4} = \frac{12}{100}$	12%	0.12
D. $\frac{1\cdot50}{2\cdot50} = \frac{50}{100}$	50%	0.5	I. $\frac{20\cdot4}{25\cdot4} = \frac{80}{100}$	80%	0.8
E. $\frac{1\cdot2}{50\cdot2} = \frac{2}{100}$	2%	0.02	J. $\frac{1\cdot5}{20\cdot5} = \frac{5}{100}$	5%	0.05

Part 2: Use **division** to convert fractions to decimals and percentages.

Fraction to Decimal	Percentage	Fraction to Decimal	Percentage
K. $\frac{1}{8}$ .125 8)1.000 −8 20 −16 40 −40	12.5%	N. Use division. $\frac{3}{6}$ .5 6)3.0 −30	50%
L. $\frac{2}{8}$ .25 8)2.00 −16 40 −40	25%	O. Simplify first, then use division. $\frac{2}{8}\frac{1}{2}$ .5 2)1.0 −10	50%
M. $\frac{3}{8}$ .375 8)3.000 −24 60 −56 40 −40	37.5%	P. Simplify first, then use a <u>proportion</u>. $\frac{3}{6}\frac{1\cdot50}{2\cdot50} = \frac{50}{100}$	50%

14   Making Sense of Conversions | © ironboxeducation.com | Log in for demo videos.

Lesson 5: Converting Decimals and Percentages to Fractions

Name_____

Fraction

Decimal ⟷ Percentage

Part 1: Factor.

```
100
 1 · 100
 2 · 50
 4 · 25
 5 · 20
10 · 10
```

Part 2: Follow along with your instructor to review the divisibility rules.

Divisor	Divisibility Rule
2	ends in 2, 4, 6, 8, or 0
4	last two digits are divisible by 4
5	ends in 5 or 0
10	ends in 0
20	ends in 20, 40, 60, 80, or 00
25	ends in 25, 50, 75, or 00 (Think 25¢, 50¢, 75¢, $1.00)
50	ends in 50 or 00
100	ends in 00

Part 3: Convert percentages and decimals to fractions, then *simplify*. (If you get stuck working with large numbers, see if you can divide by 10 to make the numbers more manageable.)

	Percentage	Fraction
A.	50%	$\frac{50}{100} = \frac{1}{2}$
B.	25%	$\frac{25}{100} = \frac{1}{4}$
C.	80%	$\frac{80}{100} = \frac{4}{5}$
D.	70%	$\frac{70}{100} = \frac{7}{10}$
E.	75%	$\frac{75}{100} = \frac{3}{4}$
F.	55%	$\frac{55}{100} = \frac{11}{20}$
G.	20%	$\frac{20}{100} = \frac{1}{5}$
H.	16.1%	★ $\frac{16.1}{100}$ $\frac{161}{1000}$

	Decimal	Fraction
I.	0.06	$\frac{6}{100} = \frac{3}{50}$
J.	0.6	$\frac{6}{10} = \frac{3}{5}$
K.	0.24	$\frac{24}{100} = \frac{6}{25}$
L.	0.2	$\frac{2}{10} = \frac{1}{5}$
M.	0.08	$\frac{8}{100} = \frac{2}{25}$
N.	0.8	$\frac{8}{10} = \frac{4}{5}$
O.	0.5	$\frac{5}{10} = \frac{1}{2}$
P.	0.501	★ $\frac{501}{1000}$

Key Points from Demo Video – Lesson 5
Converting Decimals and Percentages to Fractions

Now that students can convert from a fraction to a decimal and a percentage, they will reverse the process. They start with decimals and percentages and convert them back to fractions.

Part 1 reviews the factors of 100, which are essential for converting by using a proportion out of 100.

In Part 2, students review the divisibility rules. These are needed because after students convert a percentage or decimal to a fraction, they must simplify it. Knowing your divisibility rules makes this process easier.

In Part 2, students convert percentages and decimals to fractions, then they simplify.

The percentage 50% is converted to 50/100, which simplifies to 1/2.

The decimal 0.06 is converted to 6/100, which simplifies to 3/50.

Be careful with the starred problems. 16.1% is equal to 161/1000, and 0.501 is equal to 501/1000.

KEY LESSON

Lesson 6: Batting Averages

Name_____

Fraction

Decimal ⟶ Percentage

Directions: Follow along with your instructor to complete this lesson.

In baseball, an *"at bat"* is when it's a player's turn to bat against a pitcher. A player earns a *"hit"* when he or she hits a fair ball and reaches at least first base safely. ("Walks" don't count as "at bats," and "errors" don't count as "hits.")

The *batting average* is the number of hits divided by the number of at bats. Batting averages are usually written to three decimal places (the thousandths place value) but pronounced without saying "thousandths."

Greg, Hannah, Iris, Javier, Kevin, and Larry play on a baseball team. So far, they have the statistics shown below.

	Greg	Hannah	Iris	Javier	Kevin	Larry
Hits	2	4	3	1	2	3
At Bats	7	9	5	4	9	8
A. Write the batting average as a fraction.	$\frac{2}{7}$	$\frac{4}{9}$	$\frac{3}{5}$	$\frac{1}{4}$	$\frac{2}{9}$	$\frac{3}{8}$
B.	With your partner, decide which player has the highest batting average. Defend your answer.					
C. Convert the batting averages from fractions to decimals (round to three decimal places).	$\frac{2}{7} \approx .286$	$\frac{4}{9} \approx .444$	$\frac{3}{5} = .600$	$\frac{1}{4} = .250$	$\frac{2}{9} \approx .222$	$\frac{3}{8} = .375$
D.	Who had the highest batting average? Iris Who had the lowest batting average? Kevin These batting averages were easier to compare as decimals instead of as fractions.					
E. Convert the batting averages to percentages (to one decimal place).	28.6%	44.4%	60%	25%	22.2%	37.5%

Long division work for row C:

- Greg: 7)2.000 = .2857 (−14, 60, −56, 40, −35, 50, −49)
- Hannah: 9)4.000 = .4444 (−36, 40, −36, 40, −36, 40, −36)
- Iris: 5)3.0 = .6 (−30)
- Javier: 4)1.000 = .25 (−8, 20, −20)
- Kevin: 9)2.000 = .2222 (−18, 20, −18, 20, −18, 20, −18)
- Larry: 8)3.000 = .375 (−24, 60, −56, 40, −40)

Key Points from Demo Video – Lesson 6
Batting Averages

Lesson 6 is a key lesson, and it is the sister lesson to Lesson 1. Instead of working with test results as they did in Lesson 1, students will work with batting averages in baseball to see another example of why conversions matter.

The table shows the number of "hits" and "at bats" that each player had. Students write each player's batting average (hits ÷ at bats) on line A.

On line B, students will find that these batting averages are difficult to compare as fractions because the they have different denominators (the players have different numbers of at bats).

In Lesson 1, students were able to use a proportion to convert each fraction into an equivalent fraction out of 100. Students will not be able to do so in this lesson because the number of at bats are not all factors of 100 (the fractions' denominators are 7, 9, 5, 4, 9, and 8). Instead, students will use long division to convert to a decimal.

In line D, it's now easier to compare batting averages as decimals. In line E, students convert decimals into percentages.

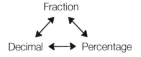

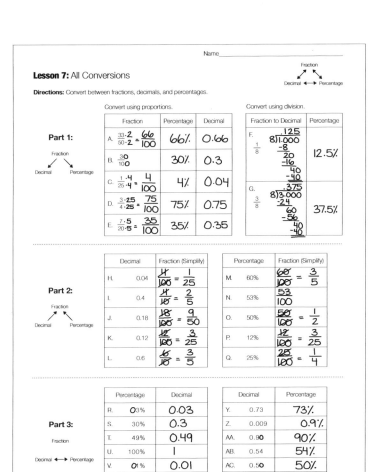

Key Points from Demo Video – Lesson 7
All Conversions

In Lesson 7, students will use all the conversions that they have learned between fractions, decimals, and percentages.

Fraction
Decimal ←→ Percentage

Part 1 involves converting fractions into decimals and percentages. Students will use proportions or long division to make these conversions.

Part 2 reverses the conversions. Students convert decimals and percentages into fractions. Students must remember that after converting to a fraction, they must simplify their answers.

Part 3 involves converting back and forth between decimals and percentages.

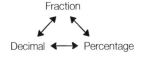

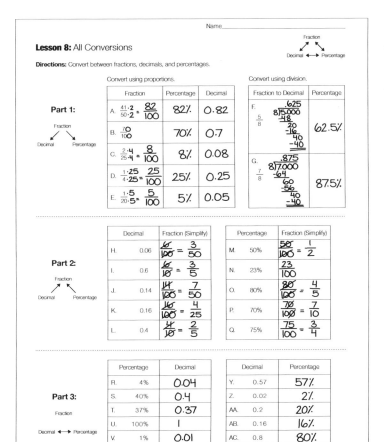

Key Points from Demo Video – Lesson 8
All Conversions

In Lesson 8, students will use all the conversions that they have learned between fractions, decimals, and percentages.

Fraction
Decimal ←→ Percentage

Part 1 involves converting fractions into decimals and percentages. Students will use proportions or long division to make these conversions.

Part 2 reverses the conversions. Students convert decimals and percentages into fractions. Students must remember that after converting to a fraction, they must simplify their answers.

Part 3 involves converting back and forth between decimals and percentages.

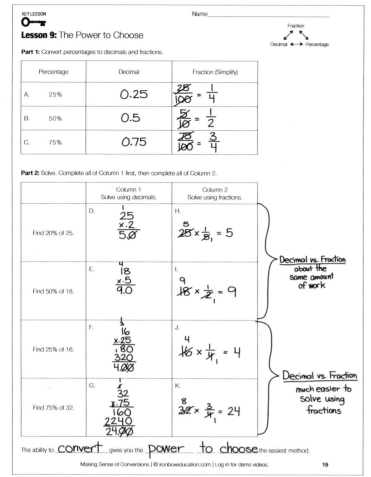

Lesson 9: The Power to Choose

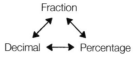

Fraction

Decimal ◀——▶ Percentage

Part 1: Convert percentages to decimals and fractions.

	Percentage	Decimal	Fraction (Simplify)
A.	25%	0.25	$\frac{25}{100} = \frac{1}{4}$
B.	50%	0.5	$\frac{5}{10} = \frac{1}{2}$
C.	75%	0.75	$\frac{75}{100} = \frac{3}{4}$

Part 2: Solve. Complete all of Column 1 first, then complete all of Column 2.

	Column 1 Solve using decimals.	Column 2 Solve using fractions.
Find 20% of 25.	D. $\begin{array}{r} 25 \\ \times .2 \\ \hline 5.0 \end{array}$	H. $25 \times \frac{1}{5} = 5$
Find 50% of 18.	E. $\begin{array}{r} 18 \\ \times .5 \\ \hline 9.0 \end{array}$	I. $18 \times \frac{1}{2} = 9$
Find 25% of 16.	F. $\begin{array}{r} 16 \\ \times .25 \\ \hline 80 \\ 320 \\ \hline 4.00 \end{array}$	J. $16 \times \frac{1}{4} = 4$
Find 75% of 32.	G. $\begin{array}{r} 32 \\ \times .75 \\ \hline 160 \\ 2240 \\ \hline 24.00 \end{array}$	K. $32 \times \frac{3}{4} = 24$

Decimal vs. Fraction about the same amount of work

Decimal vs. Fraction much easier to solve using fractions

The ability to __convert__ gives you the __power to choose__ the easiest method.

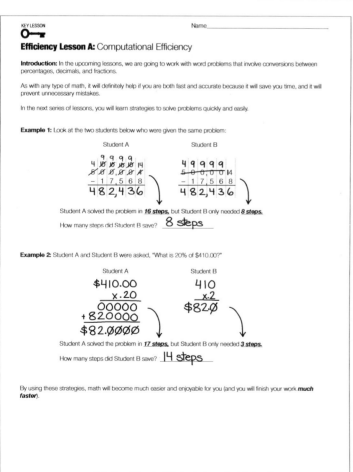

Efficiency Lesson A: Computational Efficiency

Introduction: In the upcoming lessons, we are going to work with word problems that involve conversions between percentages, decimals, and fractions.

As with any type of math, it will definitely help if you are both fast and accurate because it will save you time, and it will prevent unnecessary mistakes.

In the next series of lessons, you will learn strategies to solve problems quickly and easily.

Example 1: Look at the two students below who were given the same problem:

Student A

Student B

$$\begin{array}{r} 482,436 \end{array}$$

Student A solved the problem in **16 steps,** but Student B only needed **8 steps.**

How many steps did Student B save? ___8 steps___

Example 2: Student A and Student B were asked, "What is 20% of $410.00?"

Student A

$$\begin{array}{r} \$410.00 \\ \times .20 \\ \hline 00000 \\ +820000 \\ \hline \$82.0000 \end{array}$$

Student B

$$\begin{array}{r} 410 \\ \times .2 \\ \hline \$82.0 \end{array}$$

Student A solved the problem in **17 steps,** but Student B only needed **3 steps.**

How many steps did Student B save? ___14 steps___

By using these strategies, math will become much easier and enjoyable for you (and you will finish your work **much faster**).

Key Points from Demo Video – Lesson 9
The Power to Choose

Fraction

Decimal ◀——▶ Percentage

Now that students can easily convert between fractions, decimals, and percentages, they will learn why it's powerful to be able to do so.

In Part 1, students convert from percentages to decimals and fractions.

In Part 2, students solve "percentage of" problems first by using decimals, then by using fractions. Complete all of Column 1 first (solve using decimals), then complete all of Column 2 (solve using fractions).

The first two problems are, "Find 20% of 25," and, "Find 50% of 18." Notice that whether you multiply by decimals or multiply by fractions, the amount of work is about the same.

The last two problems are, "Find 25% of 16," and, "Find 75% of 32." **Notice that these problems are much easier to solve using fractions instead of decimals.** The ability to convert easily between percentages, fractions, and decimals gives you the power to choose the form that works best.

Computational Efficiency – Lesson A
Computational Efficiency

In upcoming lessons, students will be working with problems that involve conversions between fractions, decimals, and percentages.

As with any type of math, it will definitely help if students are both fast and accurate because it will save them time, and it will help them prevent unnecessary mistakes.

This book includes seven computational efficiency lessons (Lessons A, B, C, D, E, F, and G). These computational efficiency lessons will make students' lives easier when they work on problems involving conversions.

Example 1 shows how two students (Student A and Student B) solved the same subtraction problem in two different ways. Student A needed 16 steps, but Student B only needed 8 steps.

Example 2 shows how two students solved a decimal multiplication problem. Student A needed 17 steps, but Student B only needed 3 steps.

By learning about computational efficiency, math will become much easier and enjoyable for students.

Efficiency Lesson B: The Simple Way to Subtract with Zeroes

Part 1: Follow along with you instructor to solve the two subtraction problems below using Method 1 (standard regrouping) and Method 2 (shortcut for regrouping when subtracting with zeroes).

Method 1   Method 2

−17,568 = 482,436   −17,568 = 482,436

Part 2: Solve using the shortcut for regrouping when subtracting with zeroes. Be sure to use your pencil tip to **"touch and protect"** the number that you are subtracting from so that you don't accidentally cross it out.

Careful! Touch and protect the 0 in the ones place value so you don't cross it out accidentally.

−17,568 = 582,481   −17,568 = 782,432   −17,568 = 461,441   −17,568 = 602,432

Part 3: Subtract. When regrouping, be sure you write a number above every place value that you cross out. For example, when you cross out three digits in "100" in the first problem, replace those three digits with "099" instead of just "99" (which has only two digits).

−17,568 = 333,432   −17,568 = 683,435   −17,568 = 192,432   −17,568 = 383,432

Part 4: Subtract.

−17,568 = 582,732   −17,568 = 83,441   −17,568 = 789,432   −17,568 = 397,641

24   Making Sense of Conversions | © ironboxeducation.com | Log in for demo videos.

Efficiency Lesson C: Trailing Zeroes

When adding or subtracting decimals, the decimal points must line up so that the place values line up. But why?

Think back to the Apples Plus Apples lesson in *Making Sense of Fractions*. Thirds can only be added with thirds, just like apples can only be added with apples. It does not make sense to add things with different names such as pencils and cars.

1 third + 1 third = 2 thirds
1 apple + 1 apple = 2 apples
3 pencils + 2 cars = ~~3 pencils + 2 cars~~

The same logic applies when working with place value. The billions place value can only be added with the billions place value, the hundredths place value can only be added with the hundredths place value, and so on.

4 billion + 1 billion = 5 billion
3 hundredths + 2 hundredths = 5 hundredths

When adding or subtracting decimals, the place values have to line up. The best way to make sure the place values line up is to make sure the decimal points line up.

To make it easier to line up the decimal points when adding decimals, use trailing zeroes so that each addend has the same number of digits after the decimal point.

Part 1: When *adding or subtracting decimals*, use trailing zeroes as necessary so that each number has the same number of digits after the decimal point. Rewrite each problem in the working space, then solve. Write your final answer without trailing zeroes.

5.000 + 2.231 = 7.231   5.000 − 2.231 = 2.769

5.000 + 2.231 = 7.231   5.000 − 2.231 = 2.769

Part 2: When *multiplying decimals*, you do not need to line up the decimal points (since you're not adding or subtracting). So, should we keep trailing zeroes or should we omit them?

Solve each problem using the two methods below to find out. Remember to write your decimal point in your product correctly (if the two factors had five decimal places combined, you product should have five decimal places as well). Write your final answer without trailing zeroes.

Method 1
Keep trailing zeroes when multiplying decimals.

5.00 × 2.231 = 11.155

Method 2
Omit trailing zeroes when multiplying decimals.

5.00 × 2.231 = 11.155

In order to save **time** and reduce **errors**, we should **omit** trailing zeroes when multiplying decimals.

Making Sense of Conversions | © ironboxeducation.com | Log in for demo videos.   25

Computational Efficiency – Lesson B
Simplifying Subtraction with Zeroes

One thing that frustrates students when they're subtracting is when they have to deal with zeroes in the minuend, or the number from which another number is subtracted. The zeroes complicate things, so Lesson B shows students how to vastly simplify the process.

In Part 1, the answer key and the demo video show two methods of solving the same subtraction problem with multiple zeroes in the minuend.

Method 1   Method 2

500004 − 17568 = 482,436   500004 − 17568 = 482,436

Here's the key, as shown in the demo video. Instead of regrouping the zeroes one place value at a time (which is time-consuming and error prone), use a single stroke to regroup them all at once.

Part 2 shows that when using this technique, you must **"touch and protect"** the number you are subtracting from so that you don't accidentally cross it off. Part 3 explains the nuance of making sure to write a number over every place value you cross off.

Computational Efficiency – Lesson C
Trailing Zeroes

When adding, subtracting, or multiplying, trailing zeroes can either make your life simpler, or they can completely get in the way.

In Lesson C, students will learn to use or omit trailing zeroes effectively.

This lesson starts of having students recall the "Apples Plus Apples" lesson from the book, *Making Sense of Fractions*. In that lesson, students learned that you can only add things together if they have the same name (such as apples plus apples).

This "same name" concept applies to fractions (you can only add thirds with thirds), and it also applies to place value (you can only add billions with billions).

Part 1 shows that <u>when adding or subtracting decimals,</u> the best way to line up place value names is to make sure the decimals line up. **Use trailing zeroes** to make sure the decimal points line up.

Part 2 sows that <u>when multiplying decimals,</u> the decimal points don't need to line up (since you're not adding or subtracting). **Omit trailing zeroes** when multiplying decimals.

Efficiency Lesson D: Trailing Zeroes

Directions: Each problem in each row uses the same two numbers. Use the working space to add, subtract, or multiply as indicated. Use or omit trailing zeroes appropriately. Final answers should have no trailing zeroes.

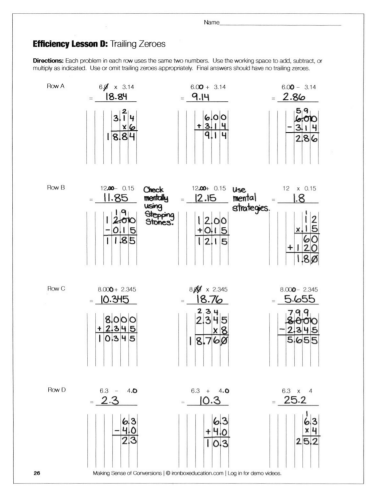

Row A

6.0 x 3.14
= 18.84

6.00 + 3.14
= 9.14

6.00 – 3.14
= 2.86

Row B

12.00 – 0.15
= 11.85   Check mentally using Stepping Stones.

12.00 + 0.15
= 12.15   Use mental strategies.

12 x 0.15
= 1.8

Row C

8.000 + 2.345
= 10.345

8.00 x 2.345
= 18.76

8.000 – 2.345
= 5.655

Row D

6.3 – 4.0
= 2.3

6.3 + 4.0
= 10.3

6.3 x 4
= 25.2

Computational Efficiency – Lesson D
Trailing Zeroes

In Lesson D, students learn to recognize situations involving trailing zeroes, and they practice using them effectively.

The problems in each row use the same two numbers, and only the operations change between them. In Row A, for example, the problems are:

- 6.0 x 3.14
- 6.0 + 3.14
- 6.0 – 3.14

Students need to remember the following:

- When adding or subtracting decimals, use trailing zeroes to line up the decimal points.
- When multiplying decimals, omit the trailing zeroes because it's not necessary to line up the decimal points or place values (since you're not adding or subtracting).

Students should use the working space to perform their calculations, and their final answers should omit trailing zeroes, as shown in the answer key.

Efficiency Lesson E: Trailing Zeroes

Directions: Each problem in each row uses the same two numbers. Use the working space to add, subtract, or multiply as indicated. Use or omit trailing zeroes appropriately. Final answers should have no trailing zeroes.

Row A

5.0 x 3.14
= 15.7

5.00 + 3.14
= 8.14   Use mental strategies.

5.00 – 3.14
= 1.86   Check mentally using Stepping Stones.

Row B

18.00 – 0.20
= 17.8

18.0 + 0.20
= 18.2

18 x 0.20
= 3.6

Row C

9.00 + 8.83
= 17.83

9.0 x 8.83
= 79.47

9.00 – 8.83
= 0.17

Row D

23.00 – 0.15
= 22.85

23.00 + 0.15
= 23.15

23.00 x 0.15
= 3.45

Computational Efficiency – Lesson E
Trailing Zeroes

In Lesson E, students learn to recognize situations involving trailing zeroes, and they practice using them effectively.

The problems in each row use the same two numbers, and only the operations change between them. In Row D, for example, the problems are:

- 23.00 – 0.15
- 23.00 + 0.15
- 23.00 x 0.15

Students need to remember the following:

- When adding or subtracting decimals, use trailing zeroes to line up the decimal points.
- When multiplying decimals, omit the trailing zeroes because it's not necessary to line up the decimal points or place values (since you're not adding or subtracting).

Students should use the working space to perform their calculations, and their final answers should omit trailing zeroes, as shown in the answer key.

Efficiency Lesson F: Calculating 15% Easily Without Multiplying

Part A: The value 15% is a useful percentage in real life. For example, it's often used for calculating tip at a restaurant. However, calculating 15% by multiplying involves a lot of steps, as you'll see below.

$$\begin{array}{r} 8\;0 \\ \times\;1\;.\;5 \\ \hline 4\;0\;0 \\ +\;8\;0\;0 \\ \hline 1\;2\;.\;0\;0 \end{array}$$ 15% of 80 is __12__

Part B: Since calculating 15% by multiplying involves a lot of work, let's break it up (decompose it) into two easier steps that you'll frequently be able to do in your head.

Easy Step 1 Calculate 10% in your head. **Easy Step 2** Calculate 5% in your head. Add Step __1__ and Step __2__ together in your head, and you'll have the answer.

Part C: Calculating 10% of a number is easy to do in your head. To find out how, calculate 10% of 80 using multiplication. Then, figure out how to get the answer in your head without multiplying.

$$\begin{array}{r} 8\;0 \\ \times\;1 \\ \hline 8\;.\;0 \end{array}$$

10% of 80 is __8__

How do you find 10% of 80 without multiplying?

Move the decimal point one space to the __left__.

Part D: To find 15% of a number without multiplying, follow these steps:

- Find 10% of the number.
- Find 5% of the number **(5% is half of 10%).**
- Add the 10% part with the 5% part to get 15%.

Without multiplying, find the answer to our original problem in Part A. Remember, **5% is half of 10%.**

15% of 80 = __12__	
10% → __8__ +5% → __+4__ 15% → __12__	Your final answer from **Part A** was __12__. Your final answer from **Part D** was also __12__, but notice how you could do the calculations in your head.

Now try these other easy examples below, and notice how you can do the calculations in your head.

15% of 500 = __75__	15% of 120 = __18__	15% of 4,000 = __600__	15% of 20,000 = __3,000__
10% → __50__ +5% → __+25__ 15% → __75__	10% → __12__ +5% → __+6__ 15% → __18__	10% → __400__ +5% → __+200__ 15% → __600__	10% → __2,000__ +5% → __+1,000__ 15% → __3,000__

28   Making Sense of Conversions | © ironboxeducation.com | Log in for demo videos.

Efficiency Lesson G: Hanging Zeroes

Part 1: Follow along with your instructor to solve the multiplication problem below using Methods 1, 2, and 3.

Method 1
$$\begin{array}{r} 6\;0\;0 \\ \times\;5\;0 \\ \hline 0\;0\;0 \\ +\;3\;0\;0\;0\;0 \\ \hline 3\;0\,,\;0\;0\;0 \end{array}$$

Method 2
$$\begin{array}{r} 6\cancel{0}0 \\ \times\;5\cancel{0} \\ \hline 30,000 \end{array}$$

Method 3
$$600 \times 50 = 30,000$$

Part 2: Solve using the Hanging Zeroes shortcut.

A. 4 x 600 =2,400	B. 300 x 5 =1,500	C. 500 x 200 =100,000	D. 4 x 5,000 =20,000
		Be careful!	Be careful!
E. 34 x 1,000 =34,000	F. 200 x 2,500 =500,000	G. 26 x 800 =20,800 $\begin{array}{r}4\\26\\\times 8\\\hline 208\end{array}$	H. 18,000 x 20 =360,000
I. 60 x 60 =3,600	J. 60 x 60 x 3 =10,800 $\begin{array}{r}1\\36\\\times 3\\\hline 108\end{array}$	K. 5 x 60 x 60 =18,000	L. 24 x 60 x 60 =86,400 $\begin{array}{r}2\\24\\\times 6\\\hline 144\\\times 6\\\hline 864\end{array}$

Part 3: Multiply by powers of 10.

M. 600 x 100 =60,000	N. 34 x 1,000 =34,000	O. 270 x 10,000 =2,700,000	P. 25 x 100,000 =2,500,000

Making Sense of Conversions | © ironboxeducation.com | Log in for demo videos.   29

Computational Efficiency – Lesson F
Calculating 15% Easily Without Multiplying

The value 15% is very useful in real life. For example, the customary tip at a restaurant is 15%.

However, calculating 15% by multiplying can be cumbersome, so Lesson F will show students how to perform this calculation in their heads without multiplying.

In Part A, students multiply decimals to find 15% of 80.

Finding 15% of 80 by multiplying decimals involves a lot of work. Parts B, C, and D show students how to break up this problem (decompose it) into easier steps that they'll frequently be able to do in their heads:

- Find 10% of the number.
- Find 5% of the number (5% is half of 10%).
- Add the 10% part with the 5% part to get 15%.

Computational Efficiency – Lesson G
Hanging Zeroes

In Lesson G, students will learn how to multiply efficiently when working with hanging zeroes. This way, they avoid doing unnecessary calculations, and they can finish their work faster.

The demo video shows that in Part 1, students solve the same multiplication problem of 600 x 50 in three different ways.

- Method 1 takes the longest.
- Method 2 uses the hanging zero approach in a vertically-written problem.
- Method 3 uses the hanging zero approach in a horizontally-written problem.

Methods 2 and 3, which both use hanging zeroes, are much more efficient.

In Part 2, students practice using the hanging zero approach to multiply numbers. Notice the use of checkmarks above the hanging zeroes in the problem. This helps students keep track of whether or not they have used the hanging zeroes yet.

In Part 3, students multiply numbers by powers of 10. The hanging zero approach works here as well.

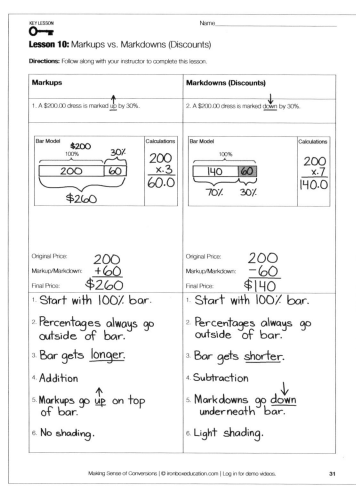

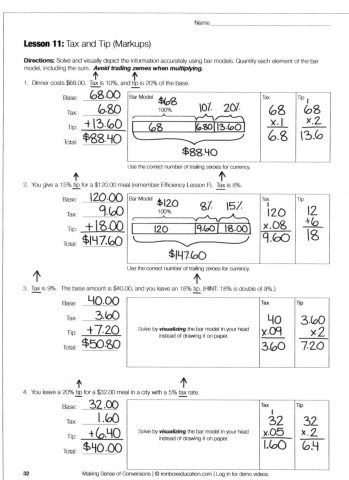

Key Points from Demo Video – Lesson 10
Markups vs. Markdowns (Discounts)

In Part 1 of this book, students learned to convert between fractions, decimals, and percentages.

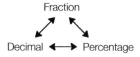

Part 2 of this book started with Computational Efficiency Lessons A, B, C, D, E, F, and G. These lessons help students work more efficiently when converting.

Starting in Lesson 10, students apply their conversion skills via markup and markdown problems, which require converting percentages into either decimals or fractions.

In this lesson, students learn to tell the difference between markups and markdowns. It's common for students to confuse these concepts. Therefore, the demo video shows students how to visually tell the difference between markups and markdowns.

Notice that throughout the upcoming lessons, students apply the conversion skills as well as the computational efficiency skills that they learned.

Key Points from Demo Video – Lesson 11
Tax and Tip (Markups)

In Lesson 11, students solve tax and tip problems, which are markup problems. These problems involve the following:

- Converting percentages to decimals.
- Multiplying decimals.
- Adding decimals.

Students solve problems 1 and 2 by visually depicting the information accurately using bar models. They should quantify each element of the bar model, including the sum. Additionally, they should avoid trailing zeroes when multiplying.

Problems 3 and 4 are solved without using a bar model. This helps students more easily make the transition from drawing a bar model on paper to eventually visualizing the bar model in their head without drawing it on paper.

Throughout the lesson, notice that the words <u>tax</u> and <u>tip</u> are underlined and are notated with an "up" arrow. Students should make these notations as a reminder that tax and tip problems all involve markups.

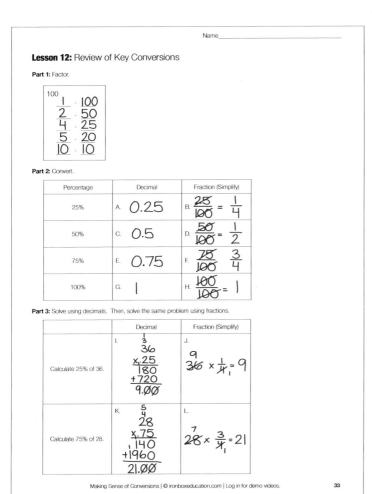

Name _____

Lesson 12: Review of Key Conversions

Part 1: Factor.

100

| 1 · 100 |
| 2 · 50 |
| 4 · 25 |
| 5 · 20 |
| 10 · 10 |

Part 2: Convert.

Percentage	Decimal	Fraction (Simplify)
25%	A. 0.25	B. $\frac{25}{100} = \frac{1}{4}$
50%	C. 0.5	D. $\frac{50}{100} = \frac{1}{2}$
75%	E. 0.75	F. $\frac{75}{100}$ $\frac{3}{4}$
100%	G. 1	H. $\frac{100}{100} = 1$

Part 3: Solve using decimals. Then, solve the same problem using fractions.

	Decimal	Fraction (Simplify)
Calculate 25% of 36.	I. $\begin{array}{r}1\\36\\ \times.25\\\hline 180\\ +720\\\hline 9.\cancel{0}\cancel{0}\end{array}$	J. $\overset{9}{\cancel{36}} \times \frac{1}{\cancel{4}_1} = 9$
Calculate 75% of 28.	K. $\begin{array}{r}5\\4\\28\\ \times.75\\\hline 140\\ +1960\\\hline 21.\cancel{0}\cancel{0}\end{array}$	L. $\overset{7}{\cancel{28}} \times \frac{3}{\cancel{4}_1} = 21$

Making Sense of Conversions | © ironboxeducation.com | Log in for demo videos.   33

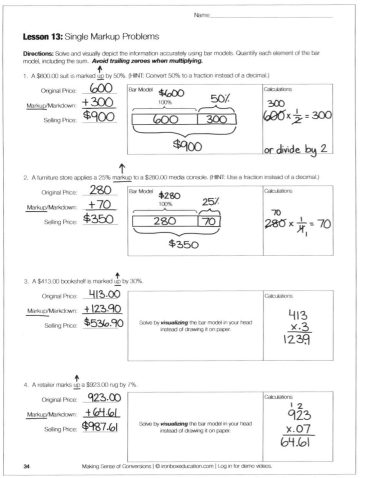

Name _____

Lesson 13: Single Markup Problems

Directions: Solve and visually depict the information accurately using bar models. Quantify each element of the bar model, including the sum. *Avoid trailing zeroes when multiplying.*

1. A $600.00 suit is marked up by 50%. (HINT: Convert 50% to a fraction instead of a decimal.)

Original Price: 600
Markup/Markdown: +300
Selling Price: $900

Bar Model $600
100% 50%
| 600 | 300 |
$900

Calculations
300
$600 \times \frac{1}{2} = 300$
or divide by 2

2. A furniture store applies a 25% markup to a $280.00 media console. (HINT: Use a fraction instead of a decimal.)

Original Price: 280
Markup/Markdown: +70
Selling Price: $350

Bar Model $280
100% 25%
| 280 | 70 |
$350

Calculations
70
$280 \times \frac{1}{\cancel{4}_1} = 70$

3. A $413.00 bookshelf is marked up by 30%.

Original Price: 413.00
Markup/Markdown: +123.90
Selling Price: $536.90

Solve by *visualizing* the bar model in your head instead of drawing it on paper.

Calculations
$\begin{array}{r}413\\ \times.3\\\hline 123.9\end{array}$

4. A retailer marks up a $923.00 rug by 7%.

Original Price: 923.00
Markup/Markdown: +64.61
Selling Price: $987.61

Solve by *visualizing* the bar model in your head instead of drawing it on paper.

Calculations
$\begin{array}{r}1\ 2\\923\\ \times.07\\\hline 64.61\end{array}$

34   Making Sense of Conversions | © ironboxeducation.com | Log in for demo videos.

Key Points from Demo Video – Lesson 11
Review of Key Conversions

Lesson 12 reviews key conversions, and it reviews the importance of Lesson 9: The Power to Choose.

In Part 1, students review the factors of 100, which will be used in Part 2.

In Part 2, students convert percentages to decimals then to fractions. Once the percentage has been converted to a fraction, students must simplify each fraction. The key conversions in Part 2, which will be used in Part 3, are:

- 25% = 1/4
- 50% = 1/2
- 75% = 3/4
- 100% = 1

Part 3 revisits Lesson 9: The Power to Choose. Students see that for problems such as, "Calculate 25% of 36," it's easier to solve by **converting 25% to a fraction** instead of a decimal.

This is why it's important to know how to fluently convert between percentages, decimals, and fractions. You have the power to choose the form of a number that works best for any situation.

Key Points from Demo Video – Lesson 13
Single Markup Problems

Lesson 13 involves single markup problems. Stores mark up the items that they sell and make them more expensive because they must be able to make a profit in order to stay in business.

Students solve problems 1 and 2 by visually depicting the information accurately using bar models. They should quantify each element of the bar model, including the sum. Additionally, they should avoid trailing zeroes when multiplying.

Problems 3 and 4 are solved without using a bar model. This helps students more easily make the transition from drawing a bar model on paper to eventually visualizing the bar model in their head without drawing it on paper.

Notice that it was easier to solve problems 1 and 2 by **converting percentages to fractions.** Problems 3 and 4 were easier to solve by **converting percentages to decimals.**

Throughout the lesson, notice that the words up and markup are underlined and are notated with an "up" arrow. Students should make these notations as a reminder that these problems involve markups.

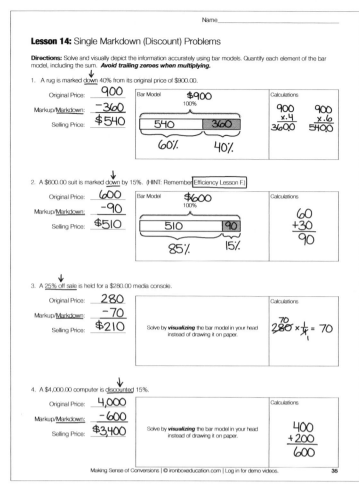

Key Points from Demo Video – Lesson 14

Single Markdown (Discount) Problems

Lesson 14 involves single markdown problems, which are also known as discounts. When an item is marked down, it goes on sale to encourage customers to purchase the item.

As was shown in the demo video for Lesson 10 (Markups vs. Markdowns), the bar model gets shorter in markdown situation. The discounted or marked-down portion of the bar model is shaded to indicate that it does <u>not</u> count toward the price of the item anymore (hence the word <u>dis</u>count).

Also, the written location of the mark<u>down</u> percentage is <u>down</u>, underneath the bar model. In a mark<u>up</u> situation, the location of the markup percentage was <u>up</u>, at the top of the bar model.

Students solve problems 1 and 2 visually with bar models. Problems 3 and 4 are solved without using a bar model. Notice that problem 3 was easier to solve by **converting the percentage to fraction** instead of a decimal.

Throughout the lesson, notice that the words indicating markdowns (<u>discounted</u>, <u>sale</u>, <u>down</u>, etc.) are underlined and notated with a "down" arrow.

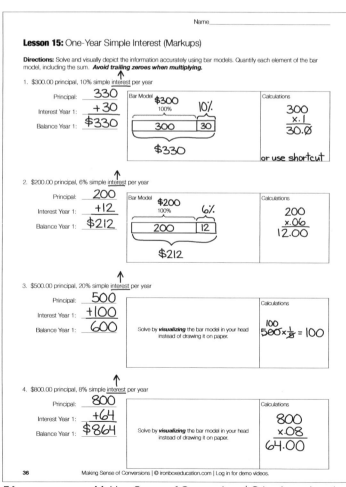

Key Points from Demo Video – Lesson 15

One-Year Simple Interest (Markups)

So far, students have worked with the following types of problems:

- Tax and tip (markups)
- Single markup
- Single markdown (discounts)

In Lesson 15, students work with one-year simple interest problems, which are markups.

Notice that the word "interest" is underlined throughout the lesson and is notated with an "up" arrow. Students should make these notations to remind them that these are markup problems.

Problems 1 and 2 are solved using a bar model. Problems 3 and 4 are solved without the use of a bar model.

Notice that problem 3 was solved more easily by **converting the percentage to a fraction** instead of a decimal.

Lesson 16: Multiple Markups

Directions: Solve and visually depict the information accurately using bar models. Quantify each element of the bar model, including the sum. *Avoid trailing zeroes when multiplying.*

1. A $280.00 media console is marked up by 25%, then marked up again by an additional 10%.

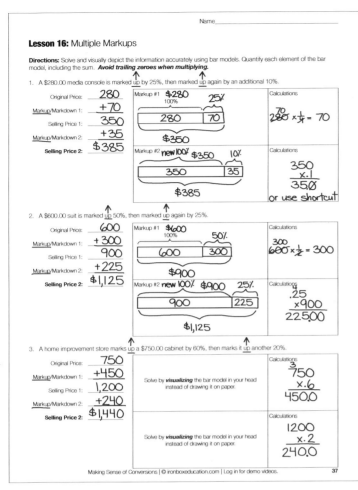

Original Price:	280
Markup/Markdown 1:	+70
Selling Price 1:	350
Markup/Markdown 2:	+35
Selling Price 2:	$385

Markup #1 $280 100% 25%
280 | 70
$350

Calculations
$280 \times \frac{1}{4} = 70$

Markup #2 new 100% $350 10%
350 | 35
$385

Calculations
350
× .1
35.0
or use shortcut

2. A $600.00 suit is marked up 50%, then marked up again by 25%.

Original Price:	600
Markup/Markdown 1:	+300
Selling Price 1:	900
Markup/Markdown 2:	+225
Selling Price 2:	$1,125

Markup #1 $600 100% 50%
600 | 300
$900

Calculations
$600 \times \frac{1}{2} = 300$

Markup #2 new 100% $900 25%
900 | 225
$1,125

Calculations
.25
× 900
225.00

3. A home improvement store marks up a $750.00 cabinet by 60%, then marks it up another 20%.

Original Price:	750
Markup/Markdown 1:	+450
Selling Price 1:	1,200
Markup/Markdown 2:	+240
Selling Price 2:	$1,440

Solve by *visualizing* the bar model in your head instead of drawing it on paper.

Calculations
750
× .6
450.0

Solve by *visualizing* the bar model in your head instead of drawing it on paper.

Calculations
1200
× .2
240.0

Lesson 17: Multiple Markdowns

Directions: Solve and visually depict the information accurately using bar models. Quantify each element of the bar model, including the sum. *Avoid trailing zeroes when multiplying.*

1. A dining table is marked down 40% from its original price of $360.00, then marked down another 20%.

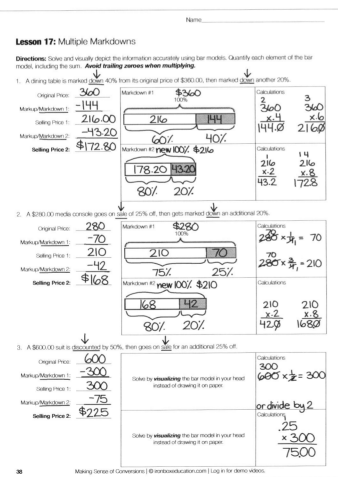

Original Price:	360
Markup/Markdown 1:	−144
Selling Price 1:	216.00
Markup/Markdown 2:	−43.20
Selling Price 2:	$172.80

Markdown #1 $360 100%
216 | 144
60% 40%

Calculations
2   3
360   360
× .4   × .6
144.0   216.0

Markdown #2 new 100% $216
178.20 | 43.20
80% 20%

Calculations
1   1 4
216   216
× .2   × .8
43.2   172.8

2. A $280.00 media console goes on sale of 25% off, then gets marked down an additional 20%.

Original Price:	280
Markup/Markdown 1:	−70
Selling Price 1:	210
Markup/Markdown 2:	−42
Selling Price 2:	$168

Markdown #1 $280 100%
210 | 70
75% 25%

Calculations
$280 \times \frac{1}{4} = 70$
$280 \times \frac{3}{4} = 210$

Markdown #2 new 100% $210
168 | 42
80% 20%

Calculations
210   210
× .2   × .8
42.0   168.0

3. A $600.00 suit is discounted by 50%, then goes on sale for an additional 25% off.

Original Price:	600
Markup/Markdown 1:	−300
Selling Price 1:	300
Markup/Markdown 2:	−75
Selling Price 2:	$225

Solve by *visualizing* the bar model in your head instead of drawing it on paper.

Calculations
300
$600 \times \frac{1}{2} = 300$

or divide by 2

Solve by *visualizing* the bar model in your head instead of drawing it on paper.

Calculations
.25
× 300
75.00

Key Points from Demo Video – Lesson 16
Multiple Markups

Now that students have had practice working with single markups and single markdowns, Lesson 16 introduces multiple markups.

Problems 1 and 2 are solved with bar models to build conceptual understanding. Problem 3 is solved without a bar model.

In problem 1, notice the two markups, as indicated by the underlines and the "up" arrows The problem reads, "A $280.00 media console is marked up by 25%, then marked up again by an additional 10%."

The problem provides space for two bar models since there are two markups.

- As shown in the demo video, Markup #1 is calculated first using the the first bar model.
- Then, the new higher selling price becomes the new 100% bar for Markup #2.

After both markups are applied, it results in the final selling price.

Notice in problem 1 that Markup #1 was easier to solve by **converting the percentage to a fraction.**

Key Points from Demo Video – Lesson 17
Multiple Markdowns

Lesson 16 covered multiple markups.

Lesson 17 covers multiple markdowns. This occurs when an item goes on sale, then the sale price is marked down further by an additional amount.

Since each problem involves two markdowns, notice that both bar models for each problem are shaded to indicate that the price is getting lower and lower.

Similar to the previous lesson, each problem provides space for two bar models since there are two markdowns.

- As shown in the demo video, Markdown #1 is calculated first using the the first bar model.
- Then, the new lower selling price becomes the new 100% bar for Markdown #2.

Notice in problem 2 that Markdown #1 was easier to solve by **converting the percentage to a fraction.**

Problem 3 is solved without the use of a bar model.

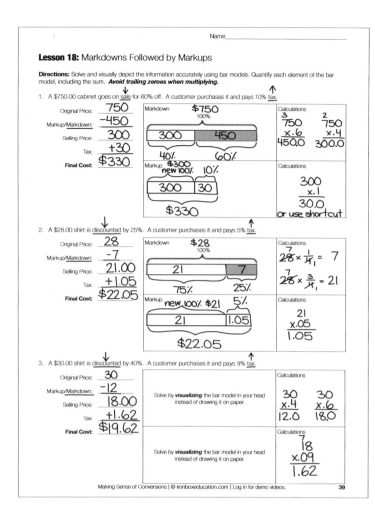

Lesson 18: Markdowns Followed by Markups

Directions: Solve and visually depict the information accurately using bar models. Quantify each element of the bar model, including the sum. *Avoid trailing zeroes when multiplying.*

1. A $750.00 cabinet goes on sale for 60% off. A customer purchases it and pays 10% tax.

Original Price:	750
Markup/Markdown:	−450
Selling Price:	300
Tax:	+30
Final Cost:	$330

Markdown $750 100%

300 | 450

40% | 60%

Calculations
3
750
x.6
450.0

2
750
x.4
300.0

Markup $300 new 100% 10%

300 | 30

$330

Calculations
300
x.1
30.0

or use shortcut

2. A $28.00 shirt is discounted by 25%. A customer purchases it and pays 5% tax.

Original Price:	28
Markup/Markdown:	−7
Selling Price:	21.00
Tax:	+1.05
Final Cost:	$22.05

Markdown $28 100%

21 | 7

75% | 25%

Calculations
$28 \times \frac{1}{4_1} = 7$

$28 \times \frac{3}{4_1} = 21$

Markup new 100% $21 5%

21 | 1.05

$22.05

Calculations
21
x.05
1.05

3. A $30.00 shirt is discounted by 40%. A customer purchases it and pays 9% tax.

Original Price:	30
Markup/Markdown:	−12
Selling Price:	18.00
Tax:	+1.62
Final Cost:	$19.62

Solve by *visualizing* the bar model in your head instead of drawing it on paper.

Calculations
30
x.4
12.0

30
x.6
18.0

Solve by *visualizing* the bar model in your head instead of drawing it on paper.

Calculations
18
x.09
1.62

Key Points from Demo Video – Lesson 18
Markdowns Followed by Markups

The previous lessons covered the following:

- Lesson 16: Multiple Markups
- Lesson 17: Multiple Markdowns

Lesson 18 covers markdowns followed by markups. This happens when a item goes on sale (markdown), someone purchases it, then pays sales tax (markup).

As in the previous two lessons, each problem has room for two bar models.

- As shown in the demo video, the markdown (discounted price) is calculated first using the the first bar model.
- Then, the new lower selling price becomes the new 100% bar for the markup (tax).

In problem 2, the markdown was easier to calculate by **converting the percentage to a fraction** instead of converting to a decimal.

Problem 3 is solved without the use of a bar model.

Lesson 19: Simple vs. Compound Interest

Directions: Solve and visually depict the information accurately using bar models. Quantify each element of the bar model, including the sum. *Avoid trailing zeroes when multiplying.*

$300.00 principal, 10% interest per year for 2 years.

SIMPLE INTEREST
Interest earned is always kept separate from the original principal. This means that the principal stays the same from year to year, and the interest earned each year stays the same as well.

Principal:	300
Interest Year 1:	+30
Balance Year 1:	330
Interest Year 2:	+30
Balance Year 2:	360

Years 1 & 2 $300 100%

300 | 30 | 30
I₁ | I₂

$360

Calculations
300
x.1
30.0

or use shortcut

Follow along with your instructor to learn the shortcut for finding the Year 2 simple interest balance.

Original Principal 100%
Year 1 Interest 10%
Year 2 Interest +10%
Final Balance 120%

120% x 300
=1.2 x 300
=360 ✓

COMPOUND INTEREST
Interest earned gets added to the principal. This means that the principal is allowed to grow larger and larger each year. Since the principal keeps getting larger and larger, the interest earned each year gets larger and larger as well.

Principal:	300
Interest Year 1:	+30
Balance Year 1:	330 ✓
Interest Year 2:	+33
Balance Year 2:	363 ✓

Year 1 $300 100% 10%

300 | 30

$330

Calculations
300
x.1
30.0

or use shortcut

Year 2 new 100% $330 10%

330 | 33
I₂

$363

Calculations
330
x.1
33.0

or use shortcut

Check the Year 1 balance and the Year 2 balance with your instructor.

Original Principal 100%
Year 1 Interest +10%
Year 1 Balance 110%

1.1
x300
330

330
x1.1
330
3300
363.0 ✓

330
x1.1
3300
330
363.0 ✓

Principal (new 100%)
+10% Interest Year 2
110% Balance Year 2

If you were earning interest, would you rather have simple interest or compound interest? **compound interest**

Key Points from Demo Video – Lesson 19
Simple vs. Compound Interest

In Lesson 15, students learned about one-year simple interest, which was a type of markup.

In Lesson 19, students learn the difference between the following:

- multi-year **simple** interest
- multi-year **compound** interest

In a **simple interest** problem, the interest earned is always kept separate from the principal. This means that the principal amount stays the same from year to year. Since the principal amount stays the same, the interest earned each year stays the same as well. In the example, the interest earned is $30 every year.

In a **compound interest** problem, the interest earned gets added to the principal. This means that the principal is allowed to grow larger and larger each year. Since the principal keeps getting larger and larger, the interest earned keeps getting larger and larger each year as well. The interest earned in year 1 is $30, then it grows to $33 in year 2.

If you were earning interest, you would rather have compound interest because you earn more.

Name_____

Lesson 20: Simple vs. Compound Interest

Directions: Solve and visually depict the information accurately using bar models. Quantify each element of the bar model, including the sum. ***Avoid trailing zeroes when multiplying.***

$500 principal, 20% interest per year for 3 years.

SIMPLE INTEREST
Interest earned is always kept separate from the original principal. This means that the principal stays the same from year to year, and the interest earned each year stays the same as well.

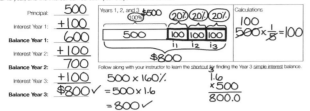

COMPOUND INTEREST
Interest earned gets added to the principal. This means that the principal is allowed to grow larger and larger each year. Since the principal keeps getting larger and larger each year, the interest earned each year gets larger and larger as well.

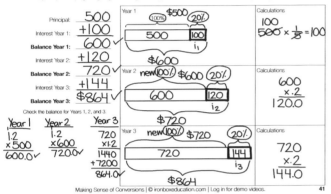

Key Points from Demo Video – Lesson 20
Simple vs. Compound Interest

In Lesson 19, students learned about the difference between simple interest and compound interest.

Lesson 20 provides another example of simple interest versus compound interest. Instead of using two years worth of earnings, Lesson 20 shows what happens when there are three years worth of earnings.

In a ***simple interest*** problem, the interest earned is always kept separate from the principal. This means that the principal amount stays the same from year to year. Since the principal amount stays the same, the interest earned each year stays the same as well. In the example, the interest earned is $100 a year, every year.

In a ***compound interest*** problem, the interest earned gets added to the principal. This means that the principal is allowed to grow larger and larger each year. Since the principal keeps getting larger and larger, the interest earned keeps getting larger and larger each year as well. The interest earned in year 1 is $100. Then, it grows to $120 in year 2 and $144 in year 3.

Making Sense of Conversions | © ironboxeducation.com | **Teachers: Log in for demo videos.**

84207500R00033

Made in the USA
San Bernardino, CA
06 August 2018